CLEM SUNTER

THE HIGH ROAD:
Where are we now?

TAFELBERG
HUMAN & ROUSSEAU

First published in 1996 jointly by
Tafelberg Publishers Ltd, 28 Wale Street, Cape Town
and Human & Rousseau (Pty) Ltd, State House,
3-9 Rose Street, Cape Town

© 1996 Tafelberg Publishers Ltd and Human & Rousseau (Pty) Ltd
All rights strictly reserved. No part of this book may be
reproduced or transmitted in any form or by any means, electronic
or mechanical, or by photocopying, recording or
microfilming, or stored in any retrieval system, without the
written permission of the publishers

Colour charts designed by Drusilla Wildgoose
and reproduced by National Book Printers
Typeset in 10.5 on 13 pt Monotype Plantin,
and printed and bound by National Book Printers,
Drukkery Street, Goodwood, Western Cape, South Africa
First edition, first impression 1996

ISBN 0 624 03527 1

TO PIERRE WACK AND TED NEWLAND
TWO OF THE GREATEST
SCENARIO THINKERS OF ALL TIME
WHO TAUGHT ME THE TOOLS
OF THE TRADE

Contents

Acknowledgements 9
Introduction 11
Methodology 11
Purpose of Scenario Thinking 14
Radar 16
Structure of Talk 17
The "Rules of the Game" 18
1. Demography 18
1.1 Impact on the Environment 19
1.2 Urbanisation and Ageing 29
1.3 Higher Savings 32
1.4 Shares of World Output 33
1.5 AIDS 35
1.6 Plagues in General 53
2. Technology 57
2.1 Kondratieff Cycles 57
2.2 Lock-In Versus Perpetual Transition 61
3. Values 68
3.1 Something for Everyone 68
3.2 Postmodernism 70
3.3 Forces Shaping Business Environment 75
3.4 Company To Believe In 79
3.5 New Reality 80
4. Summary of Rules 86
The "Key Uncertainties" 90
The Global Scenarios 96
The South African Scenarios 99

Acknowledgements

This book is based on a workshop held at the Spreadeagle Hotel in Midhurst, Sussex, in September 1995. A variety of international consultants gave us the benefit of their views. I would like to thank particularly Henry Ergas who provided an intellectually awesome overview of the forces behind the changes in the world economy; secondly, Judie Lannon who gave us a splendid and lively rendition of the new system of values spreading in the Western world; and thirdly, Edouard Parker for his unique insights on "Colombianisation". Although he wasn't at our workshop, Peter Schwartz of the Global Business Network in California was the source of the beautiful distinction between "lock-in" and "perpetual transition" industries.

The consolidation of the global material into a scenario presentation was the responsibility of Anglo's Research and Economic Services Department based in London. The main thanks for this must go to Allan Newey who heads the team. Not only did he take all the submissions to the workshop and distil them into a powerful theme, he also injected a marvellously dry sense of humour which makes any scenario presentation memorable.

Paul Missen who is a member of Allan's team made a huge contribution on the themes of the environment, biotechnology, AIDS and epidemics in general. Five years ago, he foresaw that a cocktail of drugs might lead to a breakthrough in AIDS treatment. For South African data on AIDS and many of the charts I am indebted to Jenny Crisp who advises Anglo's operating companies on programmes to combat the disease.

As far as the South African scenarios are concerned, I've used the original diagram drawn up by Michael O'Dowd and Bobby Godsell. It is truly an extraordinary feat to design a scenario model that has not only proved utterly relevant to the last ten years of South Africa's development but provides a valid framework for the next ten years as well.

I must commend my two publishers, Kerneels Breytenbach of Human & Rousseau and Lappies Labuschagne of Tafelberg, for prevailing on me to write this book. I wouldn't have done so without their encouragement. My old friend Jürgen Fomm has overseen the initial design and layout of the book. Linette Viljoen and Jill Martin have ably contributed at a more detailed level.

Finally there are the two stars who did the brunt of the work: Pat Meneghini who took down the whole manuscript in shorthand and then typed it out and Drusilla Wildgoose who was responsible for the marvellously clear and colourful graphics. Heartfelt thanks to you both.

Introduction

This little book is written to celebrate the tenth anniversary of the roadshow which I undertook with two other members of the Anglo scenario team in 1986 and 1987. Michael Spicer, Jim Buys and I crisscrossed South Africa talking to every single community that asked us to do so – 30 000 people in total. Politicians and civil servants; business people from every walk of life; farmers, doctors and journalists; academics and teachers; students and school children: we talked to them all.

The formal title of the talk as well as the book and the video that followed was *The World and South Africa in the 1990s*. However, the presentation quickly came to be known as "The High Road" after the name of the positive scenario we outlined for the country.

An appropriate interval has elapsed for us to ask: Where are we now? This book therefore provides a complete update of the material that we presented at the time. Obviously, whereas the original research took us to the turn of this century, we will now be looking further ahead to the year 2010. But, before I get into the content, I would like to revisit the methodology of scenario thinking, because some of the readers of this book may well be too young (or too old) to recall the details of the 1986 presentation.

METHODOLOGY

Chart 1 illustrates the basic presumption of scenario thinking: the world offers a universe of possibilities, any of which may materialise. A cone of uncertainty therefore opens up into the future. For example, it may be safe to say that the gold price next year could lie in a range of $100 around the present price. But in the year 2010 the range could be anything up to $1 000. This goes for virtually any parameter you care to name in a business context. Uncertainty cannot be eliminated by analysis. So it has to be embraced by whatever method you choose to look at the future.

Interestingly, business on the whole is still Newtonian in its outlook, believing that sufficient research will enable you to uncover the future workings of the world with precision and clarity. As we know, quantum physicists abandoned Isaac Newton's deterministic model at the beginning of this century in interpreting the microscopic world of electrons and other sub-atomic phenomena. Indeed, one of the fundamental axioms of quantum physics is Heisenberg's "uncertainty principle", which holds that you cannot measure with complete accuracy the position and momentum of a particle at the same time.

Scenario thinking advocates a similar approach. As a first step you try, within reason, to reduce the number of future possibilities which pertain to the system that you are examining. Hence, the narrower green cone inside the purple cone on the chart. The way you do this is by establishing the "rules of the game" that govern the system. In football, rugby or cricket, if you understand the rules you know that there is a limited range of outcomes. For instance, it is extremely unlikely that a soccer match will end

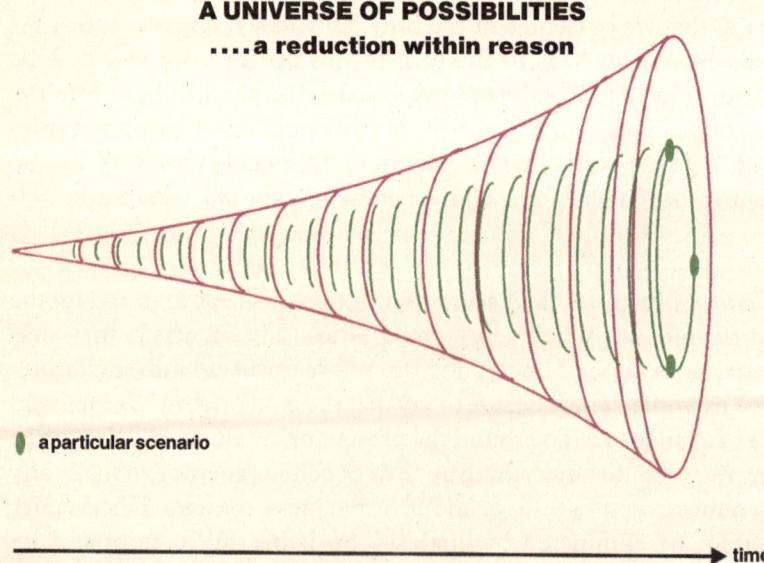

A UNIVERSE OF POSSIBILITIES
....a reduction within reason

● a particular scenario

⟶ time

Chart 1 *(Devlin)*

up with the same score as a rugby match or a rugby match as a cricket match. In this book, we will be considering the "rules of the game" that govern the world economy and to which we as a nation are subject like all other nations. Equally, businesses anywhere in the world have to play by these rules. They are beyond the control of any individual nation or business to modify.

Much of the book is spent on these rules, because some people think that they can play according to different rules and win. It doesn't happen that way in sport and it doesn't happen that way in business either. The winners are those who play best according to the rules that are in place. Where players do exercise control is over the level of skills that they develop and the strategies and techniques that they use in order to achieve victory.

This brings me to the second step in scenario thinking, which is to establish the "key uncertainties" that will drive the system you are considering in one or other direction. As you will see later, for the world as a whole we settled on two opposing forces which could drive it broadly in opposite directions in the next fifteen years. As for South Africa, having managed to make a miraculous political transition, we now face the key uncertainty of whether or not we will take the correct turning at the economic crossroads.

The third and final step is to depict the scenarios that are possible when combining the "rules of the game" with the "key uncertainties". These are represented by the three green discs on the inner cone. Notice that they are on the edge of the inner cone since they should represent futures which are at the outer realms of reasonable possibility.

A critical thing to remember is that a scenario is a story of what can happen. It is not a forecast of what is going to happen. The problem with forecasting is that we so often are deceived into forecasting our wishes and desires. I have seldom come across a strategic plan which goes against the ambitions of the CEO. We all know about hockey-stick projections where the product's demand or price is shown as flat or falling in the short term, thus giving the forecast a respectable stamp of conservatism. It then rises into the blue skies in the longer term as caution is thrown to the winds! Moreover, because forecasting has a head-on-the-block quality about it, forecasters on the whole are unwilling to use their imagination and come up with something that completely challenges contemporary thinking. They'll look foolish if they are wrong.

PURPOSE OF SCENARIO THINKING

So why does one use scenario thinking? If I haven't already convinced you, *Chart 2* gives a more specific answer: to think the unthinkable before it happens to you – either in a positive or a negative way. Let us first look at two examples where disasters happened because success made people blind to alternative possibilities.

The first example was the *Titanic*, which sank on its maiden voyage from Southampton to New York on 14/15 April 1912. In the icy North Atlantic, 1 513 souls perished on that night out of a total number of 2 224 on board. The scenario of sinkability was never played by anyone. Not by the engineers who designed the ship and did not provide a sufficient number of lifeboats. Not by the captain who, despite three warnings of icebergs in the vicinity of his boat, went full-steam ahead to meet his scheduled arrival time. Not by the passengers who, before the accident, never complained that they hadn't received a safety drill and who, after the accident, only half-filled the insufficient lifeboats that were lowered. And not by the nearby *Californian* which mistook a distress flare from the *Titanic* as a sign of a party taking place on board. As the chairman of the White Star Shipping Line said at the inquiry afterwards: "We thought the *Titanic* was a giant lifeboat in herself." Scenario thinking might have pre-empted the accident if the captain had slowed down and made course corrections. It certainly could have reduced the number of casualties.

A few years ago Barings, the oldest merchant bank in Britain, was considered as unsinkable as the *Titanic*. But this venerable institution similarly did not perceive the lethal potential of a rogue trader in the Far East who could build up a position which would ultimately sink the company. The iceberg was a 28-year-old financial whiz kid, called Nick Leeson, whose head over time

> **WHY SCENARIO THINKING?**
>
> * **To Think the Unthinkable –**
>   **BEFORE It Happens to You**
>   Negative Sense – Titanic
>   – Barings
>   Positive Sense – South Africa
>   – Microsoft
>
> * **Radar + Flight Plan =**
>   **Scenario Thinking + Strategic Planning**
>
> * **Simulator Training =**
>   **Scenario Learning**

Chart 2 *(Gallo, Neal and Sunter)*

had been turned by a string of successful trades in the market. He eventually ran up a $27 billion position on behalf of the company. This turned sour. In retrospect, if top management had played that scenario, they could have averted the incident by making the control systems covering derivatives trading much tighter, as well as by improving the procedures for screening and selecting staff. To have the same person instigating the trades and being in charge of the back-room paperwork – as Leeson was – can be classified as unforgivable.

In a positive sense, scenario thinking has been successfully used to take advantage of unthinkable opportunities when they arise. Take our own scenario team. We challenged South Africa to think the unthinkable in 1986. What if all South Africans sat down at a negotiating table to work out a new constitution peacefully, instead of having a war? What if sanctions were lifted and we got back into the world? How would we compete so that we could join others as a "winning nation"? By asking these questions, we turned the unthinkable idea of a positive future for South Africa into a possibility when all around were so utterly negative about the country's prospects. This in turn facilitated a change in direction in the national debate.

Suddenly, people started saying "why not?", and what began as a faint blip of optimism on the periphery of the radar screen became steadily brighter and spread towards the centre of the public consciousness. Nelson Mandela's release and the holding of the first democratic elections in South Africa were regarded by many as a miracle. But that is exactly why scenario thinking is so powerful. We not only captured the miracle in a scenario before it happened, but we outlined the steps to make it happen. We would never have accomplished this leap of imagination through the conventional means of forecasting and strategic planning. One has to draw the conclusion that, by considering the world as a universe of possibilities, one is much more likely to pick the right path ahead than by rigidly planning for the future.

Another fine example of the flexibility and open-mindedness required for scenario work is none other than Bill Gates, the chairman of Microsoft. He talks of going away to some retreat with his team to have radar sessions. One of these sessions recently picked up the fact that the Internet was going to be a lot more powerful and universal than his team had previously anticipated.

Microsoft executed a complete U-turn in its strategy, which is very rare for such a large company to do. It decided to abandon its plan for constructing its own Net in favour of putting all its resources behind providing software to enable easier access to the Internet and make it a more powerful tool for the user.

RADAR

The best analogy for scenario thinking is this. Pilots not only file a flight plan for their aircraft before they fly, they also have their radar switched on for the unexpected during the flight. Likewise, any company should, in addition to formulating a strategic plan, have bouts of scenario thinking to pick up deviations from the plan. You would not be appreciative as an airline passenger if the captain came over the intercom while taxiing down the runway and said: "Ladies and Gentlemen, I am so familiar with this route and the flight plan is so detailed that I am going to switch off the radar!" You would want to head for the nearest exit. But that is exactly what many companies do. They have so much confidence in their strategic plan that they switch off their radar.

Another way of highlighting the power of scenarios is to ask yourself why pilots go through simulators before they are put on actual flights. From experiencing extreme scenarios in a simulator, pilots learn very quickly what they do and they don't control. If unusual circumstances occur on actual flights, the odds are much better that they will make the correct decisions. Scenarios can do exactly the same for managers. If they rehearse their lines, they'll perform much better in the actual play.

STRUCTURE OF TALK

This book is the text of the updated talk. It is divided into two parts as indicated in *Chart 3*. The first part, which comprises the majority of the material, concerns the global scenarios produced by our scenario team in London. They are linked into an international network of remarkable people who are recognised experts in fields such as demography, technology and social values, or are specialists on particular countries like Russia, China, America and Japan.

The second part of the book deals with the unfolding of the South African scenarios prepared by our own in-house team in Johannesburg. However, as I have always said, we do not have a monopoly of the truth. Whenever I give live presentations of this material and somebody asks me a smart question that I can't answer, I modify the talk!

STRUCTURE OF TALK

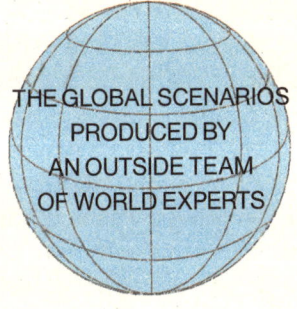

THE GLOBAL SCENARIOS
PRODUCED BY
AN OUTSIDE TEAM
OF WORLD EXPERTS

THE SOUTH AFRICAN SCENARIOS
PRODUCED BY
ANGLO IN-HOUSE RESOURCES
BUT MODIFIED DURING TALKS

Chart 3

The "Rules of the Game"

We classify the global "rules of the game" into three categories – demography, technology and social values. We shall first look at demography. This is logical since demography means people and people means customers who come first in business.

1 DEMOGRAPHY

The first chart I would like to show on demography has one of those "gee whiz" qualities about it. *Chart 4* demonstrates the incredible growth in world population in the last 100 years. We all have a vague idea about the population explosion, but the chart produced by Edouard Parker, a brilliant Frenchman who serves as a consultant to our team, reveals the true magnitude of it. The numbers on the right of the chart indicate the population in billions and the thin red

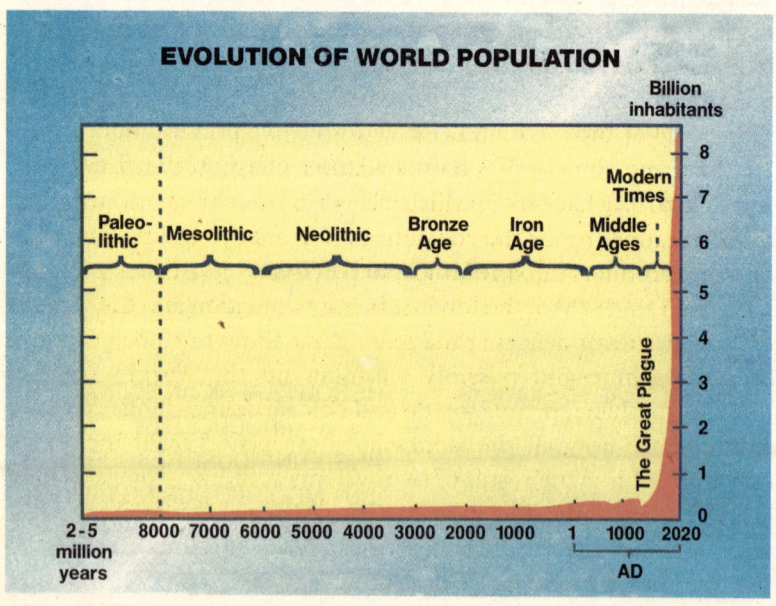

Chart 4 *(Edouard Parker)*

section across the bottom displays how it has grown since the beginning of mankind. For most of Time, the world's population has remained below 500 million. You can see the bite that the Great Plague or Black Death took out of the world's population between 1437 and 1441 when it destroyed 25 per cent of Europe's population and killed a total of 75 million people.

Global population reached its first billion in the earlier part of the nineteenth century. Then it took off. We hit the second billion in 1925, the third billion in 1962, the fourth billion in 1975 and the fifth billion in 1986. In 1996 we are now at 5,5 billion with the sixth, seventh and eighth billion marks projected to be passed in 1999, 2009 and 2019 respectively. This century is like no other one in demographic terms. The principal reason is the miracles of modern medicine cutting down on infant mortality on the one hand and extending the life expectancy of people on the other hand. In the latter regard, the life expectancy of a man in America in 1900 was 46 and is now 72 and of a woman was 48 and is now 79. As one middle-aged citizen put it: "When I was a kid 40 was middle-aged, 50 was old and 60 was dead. Now 65-year-old kids are taking care of 85-year-old parents, and a 53-year-old like me runs around a track."

1.1 IMPACT ON THE ENVIRONMENT

At the same time as we have had this incredible expansion of population, we have had industrialisation from 1750 onwards. Industrialisation means the consumption of energy and the emission of waste products into the atmosphere. *Chart 5* illustrates what has happened since 1850, the top line being population and the various lines underneath denoting the main gases thought to be polluting the atmosphere and possibly warming up the world – carbon dioxide, methane, nitrous oxide and chlorofluorocarbons (CFCs). You can see how all the slopes have steepened from the 1950s onwards. This is the result of two systems colliding – one dynamic and the other static. The dynamic one is a growing world economy and the static one is the Earth's atmosphere. The amount of air we breathe is not increasing. (Nor, for that matter, is the water we drink or the land we till.)

Chart 6 shows the increase in global temperature this century, the zero line being the average for 1951 to 1980. We have gone from a position of 0,3 degrees centigrade cooler than average in 1900 to 0,3 degrees centigrade warmer by 1990. This represents a positive change of 0,6 degrees centigrade. While this doesn't sound like much, a rise of two to three degrees centigrade will expand the water in the oceans, start melting the polar icecaps and raise the sea level. Parts of Plettenberg Bay will start disappearing as well as many low-level islands in the Pacific.

There are clear scientific grounds for believing that during this century the atmospheric concentration of man-made "greenhouse" gases has increased and at the same time global temperatures have risen. What is not yet scientifically proven is a causal link between the two charts. One hundred years is a very short period in geological time, and the rise in temperature could just be "random noise" and could easily be followed by a fall next

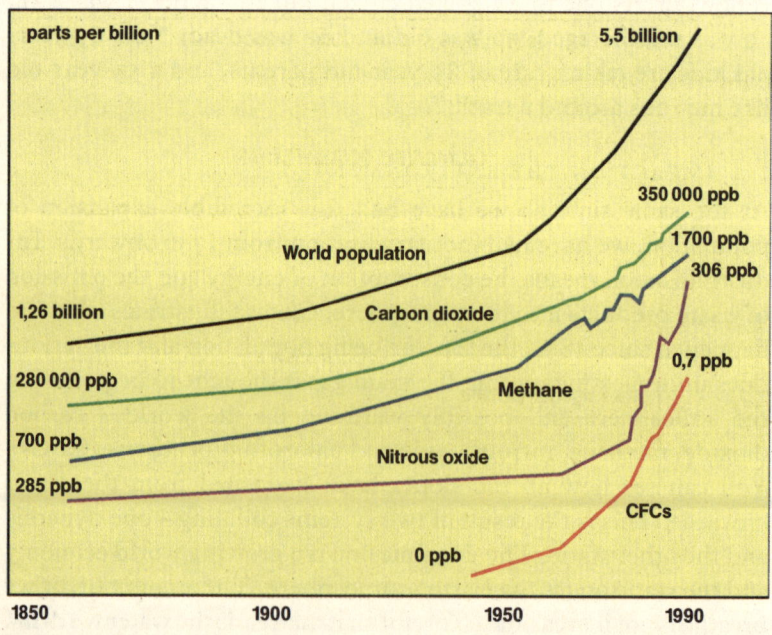

Chart 5 *(Missen)*

GLOBAL MEAN COMBINED AIR/SEA SURFACE TEMPERATURE 1900-1994

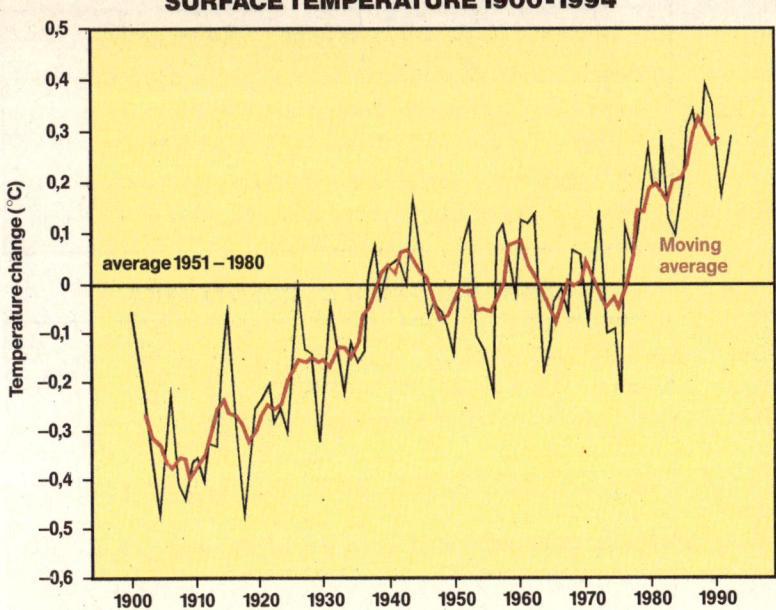

Chart 6 (Hadley Meteorological Office, UK; Dept. of Energy, US)

CLIMATE MODELLING

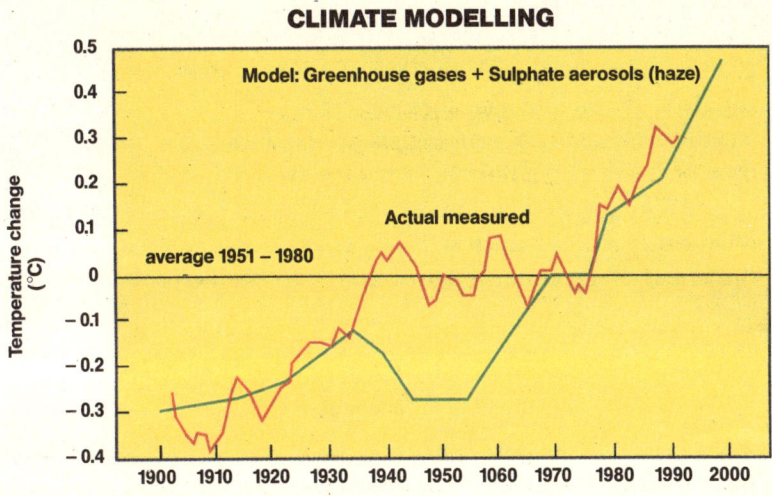

Chart 7 (Mitchell, et al., Nature, August 1995)

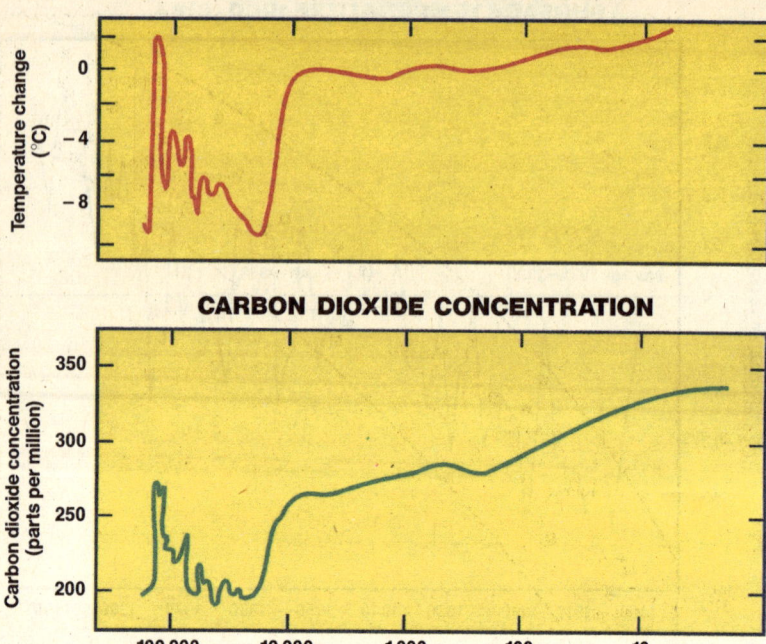

Chart 8 *(Pearman, 1988)*

century. However, with the use of super-computers and highly sophisticated mathematical reasoning and additional data on how weather is caused, climatologists are beginning to come up with models suggesting a linkage.

In *Chart 7*, we superimpose on the actual temperature change during this century the results of the latest model which combines the effect of greenhouse gases and sulphate aerosols (the latter being microscopic particles which tend to cool the world down because they reflect sunlight back into space). Apart from a period between 1930 and 1960, where the model calculates lower temperatures, the fit is beginning to look very snug indeed.

The changes in atmospheric carbon dioxide and global mean surface temperature over the past 160 000 years have also been plotted from an analysis of Antarctic ice cores. You can see the re-

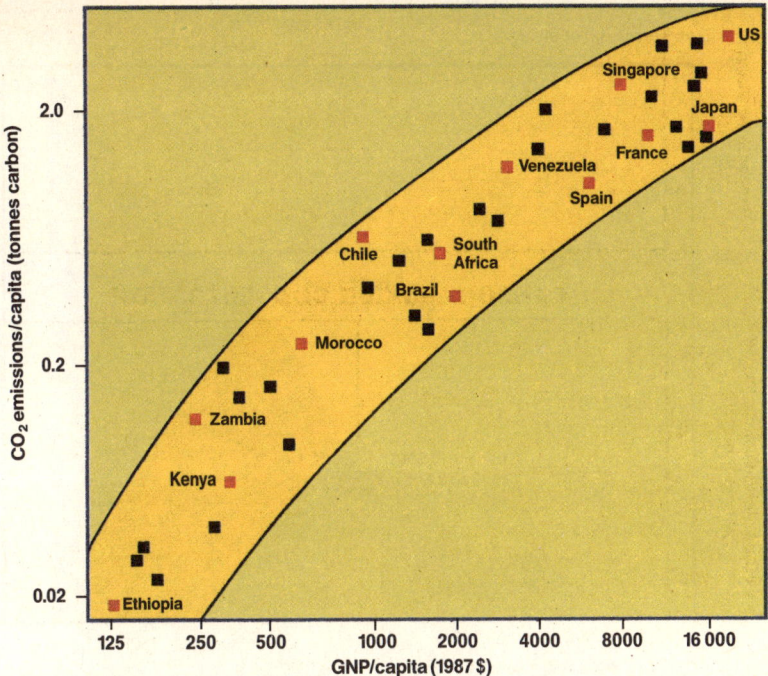

Chart 9 *(World Resources Institute)*

markable relationship in *Chart 8*. While one must stress again that the close congruence of patterns doesn't prove conclusively that past changes in the climate were induced by carbon dioxide, it does demonstrate that variations in carbon dioxide have formed an integral link with climate.

Chart 9 denotes energy as a function of income – namely the richer one is the more energy one consumes. Thus you will find the US in the top right-hand corner of the chart, South Africa in the middle and Ethiopia closest to the origin. The graph also points to the supreme quandary that the rich nations find themselves in today. Most of the 5,5 billion of the Earth's inhabitants are located in the bottom left-hand quadrant of the chart where the gradient of the energy curve is at its steepest. The reason for this is that when you are poor you cannot afford to use expensive

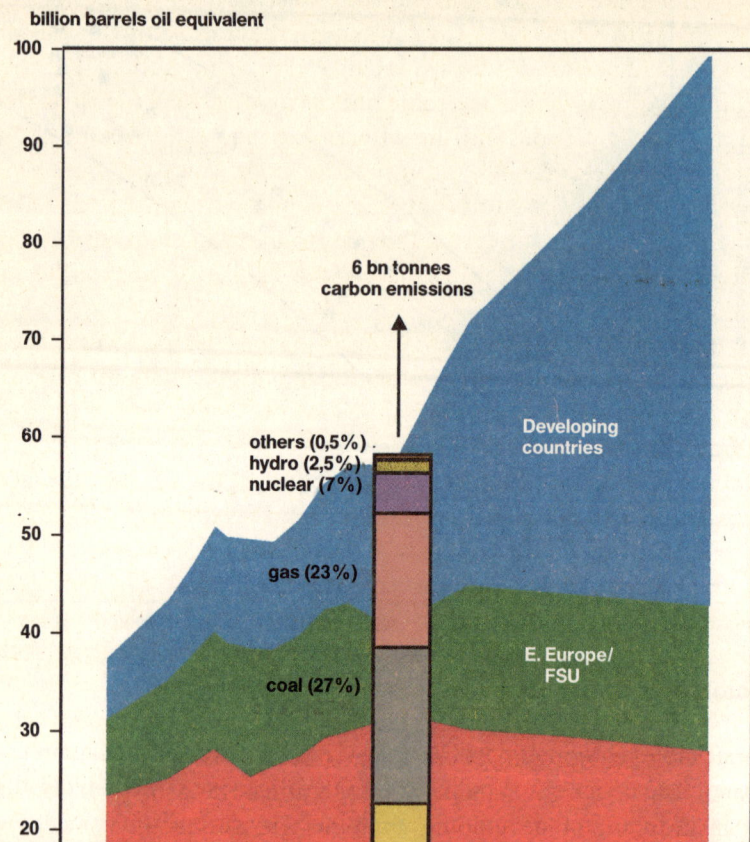

Chart 10 *(Shell International)*

energy-saving devices. It is only when you reach the upper right-hand regions of the chart that you can invest in these devices and get the curve to bend over. How, then, do the rich countries tell the poor countries (and here we include China and India) that they cannot industrialise in the same blind way that they, the rich ones, did, because it could put the whole Earth in peril through global warming? How do they compel the poor countries to follow environmentally friendly but more expensive paths of development? Won't the retort from the poor to the rich countries be: You created the mess in the first place. So subsidise us and we'll think about it.

Chart 10 puts the problem in even sharper perspective. It specifies what has happened to total global energy consumption since 1970 and projects what will happen on present trends to the year 2020. The lowest layer of red is the energy consumption attributable to countries which are members of the OECD, i.e. the Organisation for Economic Co-operation and Development. These are the rich nations and comprise Canada, the United States, Western Europe, the Scandinavian countries, Australia and New Zealand. Their growth in energy consumption from 1970 to 1996 was fairly modest. Moreover, with the latest conservation techniques, their consumption could marginally decline in future.

The next layer of green represents the former Soviet Union and Eastern Europe. There again, one doesn't see major expansion. But the blue on top, which signifies the growth in energy consumption of developing countries, is astonishing. They are coming off a very low base at present. The combination of more people plus a relatively small increase in per capita income and therefore per capita energy makes overall energy consumption rocket. Obviously, one cannot rule out the possibility that further technological progress could markedly decrease the gradient of the blue slope. However, it is hardly likely to level off like the OECD's consumption. Take cars for example, which contribute one-fifth of the carbon dioxide emissions. There were only 50 million cars in the world in 1950 and now there are 500 million – a tenfold increase. Successful developing countries are going to see a massive increase in their car population in the next century. While catalysts are able to screen out many of the noxious fumes from cars, they don't at present reduce the level of carbon dioxide emissions.

Apart from global warming, another implication of this chart is that OPEC will ride again when we enter the new century. The pillar in the middle of the chart signifies that oil at present represents 40 per cent of global energy consumption. The latest predictions are that, even with energy savings, global demand for oil could be around 92 million barrels a day in 2010 compared to 68 million barrels per day in 1994. If supply is virtually static from the rest of the world, the call on OPEC could rise from 27 million barrels per day to as many as 49 million barrels per day in 2010. OPEC, which currently has over two-thirds of the estimated reserves of oil in the world, would then be supplying 55 per cent of global oil needs. The question is whether the world will want to put so many eggs into the Middle Eastern basket. They will remember the oil price shocks of the 1970s. The alternative scenario is that the West in particular will seek much greater enhancements in energy conservation technologies in order to avoid this dependence. Substitution of oil with other energy sources must be an option too. The electric car may become a widespread reality far sooner than we currently anticipate. Ironically, it may be economics and the reduction of political risk which propels the world to take the first steps towards becoming environmentally correct. Anglo is already covering this base in terms of the Zebra project. This is a partnership with Daimler Benz to produce an "alternative petrol" in the form of an electric car battery which gives satisfactory acceleration, top speed and range – and is safe to use. Obviously, the electricity that charges the battery must come from a cleaner source too.

One important side effect of global warming must be mentioned. In a warmer world, some major tropical diseases are likely to spread and put far higher numbers of population at risk. These are listed in *Chart 11*. Malaria, for example, could increase its present prevalence of infection of 270 million to 2,1 billion people. Other diseases like schistosomiasis and filariasis will not be far behind.

The bottom line is that the issue of global warming is set to rise

MAJOR TROPICAL DISEASES LIKELY TO SPREAD IN A WARMER WORLD

	Vector	Population at risk (millions)	Present prevalence of infection (millions)	Present distribution	Likelihood of altered distribution with warming
Malaria	mosquito	2 100	270	(sub)tropics	highly likely
Schistosomiasis	water snail	600	200	(sub)tropics	very likely
Filariasis	mosquito	900	90	(sub)tropics	likely
Onchocerciasis (River blindness)	black fly	90	18	Africa/ Latin America	likely
African Trypanosomiasis (Sleeping sickness)	tsetse fly	50	25 000 new cases/year	Tropical Africa	likely
Dengue	mosquito	estimates unavailable		Tropics	very likely
Yellow Fever	mosquito	estimates unavailable		Tropical S. America & Africa	likely

Chart 11 *(World Health Organisation, The Lancet)*

on the global agenda. Moreover, although the world of science is very important, the world of perception is even more so, because that is what drives politicians to formulate their policies and enact laws and regulations. Two quotations are germane to this point. The first comes from Article 3.3, the UN Framework Convention on Climate Change, 1992: "When there are threats of serious or irreversible damage, lack of full scientific certainty should not be used as a reason for postponing measures to prevent its adverse effect." The second is a quote from Michael MacCracken, director of the US Global Change Research Programme, who said in *Nature* in August 1995: "Although greenhouse gases and aerosols are not yet convicted beyond all reasonable doubt, the case is becoming steadily stronger."

Taking these two quotations together, the momentum to wean man away from his first discovery – the use of fire – is growing. Nevertheless, the difficulties involved in such a transition are of a much greater scale than the ban on CFCs which the Montreal Protocol put in place in light of the possible depletion of the ozone layer. Most companies have been able to cope with this ban by substituting newly designed refrigerants for CFCs in air-con-

WORLD RURAL & URBAN POPULATION

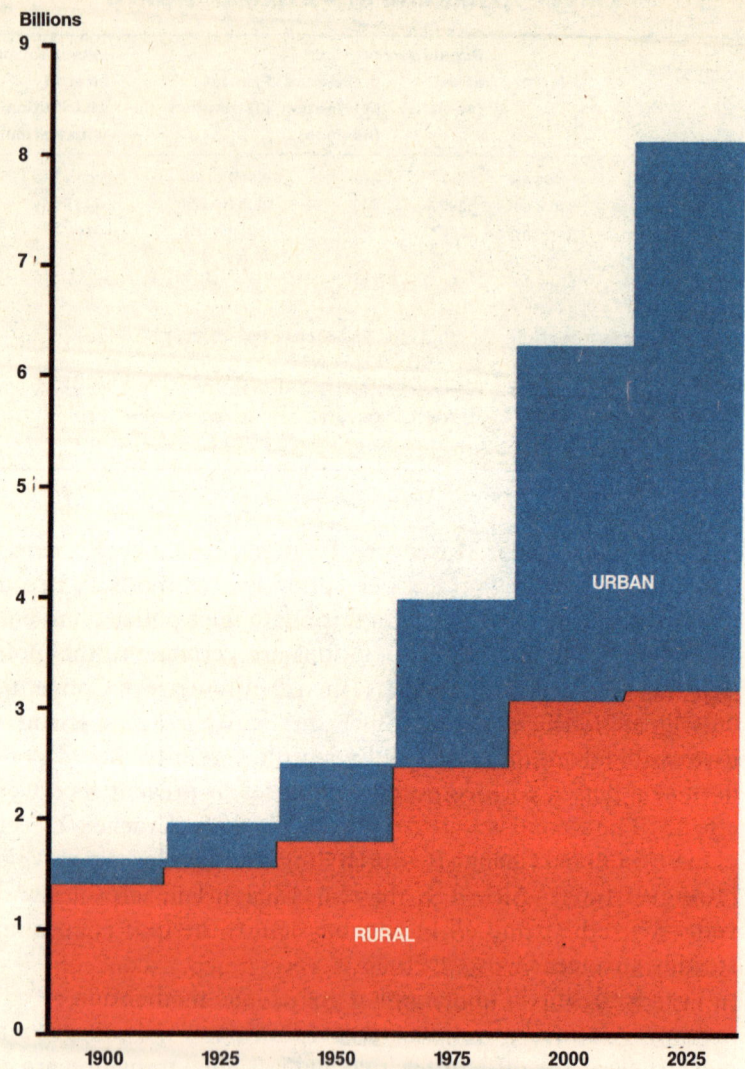

Chart 12 *(AAC Research and Economic Services Dept., London)*

ditioning equipment, the specific field where CFCs are overwhelmingly used. Carbon consumption is far more pervasive. Moving away from it will affect virtually every area of industrial activity. Thus, a serious counterproposition being raised by some scientists is that the cost of slowing the growth of greenhouse gas emissions significantly may actually exceed that of the damage caused by climatic change. Therefore, continue as is. Many ordinary citizens will find this view problematic, since it puts the habitability of Earth at stake for future generations.

I must stress that I don't want to appear Malthusian. If you remember, Thomas Malthus, a British economist and cleric, wrote the famous "Essay on the Principle of Population" in 1798, in which he maintained that population increases in a geometrical ratio, whereas the food supply increases in an arithmetical ratio. With no check on population growth, people would therefore starve and this would naturally reduce population. Malthus underestimated human ingenuity in improving agricultural methods. Likewise, the person who, before the advent of the car, prognosticated that London would be covered in horse manure fell into the trap of presuming that the future is like the past. My point is that, despite the enormous obstacles, the world will modify its behaviour if it has to. In other words, we're not going to fry – we're going to change by finding more efficient means to convert fossil fuels into electricity, by inventing new energy-saving devices and by discovering alternative energy sources.

1.2 URBANISATION AND AGEING

Chart 12 shows how much the world has urbanised since 1900. Indeed, in 1900 the world was very much a rural community. Clustering in towns and cities is very much a concept of the twentieth century. The number of people in urban areas will overtake the number in rural areas for the first time in 2000. Interestingly, we projected in our 1986 study that mega-cities like Mexico City and São Paulo would have between 25 and 30 million inhabitants. We were wrong. There is a limit to urban sprawl and mega-cities seem to have a ceiling of around 20 million (other than Tokyo, which does have 30 million because of the space constraint on the Japanese population). People are now moving to small cities and towns. They represent the fastest growing markets, which is an important point for entrepreneurs to bear in mind when deciding where to open up new businesses.

However, the leading consequence of urbanisation is that it is slowing down the global population growth rate for several reasons. Firstly, with space being more expensive, urbanised families tend to be smaller. Secondly, more women go out of the home to work in an urban environment. Thirdly, the traditional norms favouring male dominance in rural areas are eroded by the modernity of life in cities. Hence, the decision to have kids is more democratic. This diminishes the number per family since women bear the brunt of rearing children and usually want fewer than men.

Given that the world is still adding between 90 and 100 million people per year to its population, it may appear strange that population growth is decelerating. But it is, because each year's incremental number of 90 to 100 million is being divided by a larger population base.

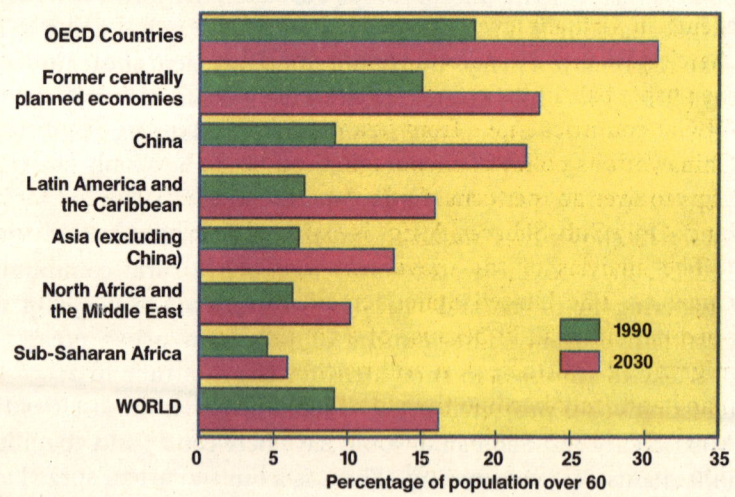

Chart 13 *(International Bank for Reconstruction and Development, 1995, "Averting the Old Age Crisis")*

OECD AGEING ANALYSIS

% of population over 60 years old	1990	2000	2010	2020	2030
US	17	17	19	25	28
Canada	16	17	20	26	30
Germany	20	24	27	30	35
France	19	20	23	27	30
UK	21	21	23	26	30
Italy	21	24	27	31	36
Japan	17	23	29	31	33
OECD weighted average	18	20	23	27	31

Chart 14 *(International Bank for Reconstruction and Development, 1995, "Averting the Old Age Crisis")*

Chart 13 shows the net result of at least half the human beings on Earth having smaller families because they live in urban areas. In contrast to this century, where the pendulum has swung towards younger populations, the next century is going to see rapid ageing in virtually every part of the world. The green bar in this chart represents the percentage of population over 60 in 1990 and the purple bar the ratio 40 years later, in 2030. You can see that the OECD countries move from just over 20 per cent to 31 per cent. China with its policy of encouraging couples to have only one child leaps to over 20 per cent. Latin America and India are not far behind. Only Sub-Saharan Africa is expected to exhibit little change.

The analysis of the movement in rich countries is given in *Chart 14*. The United States remains the youngest of the developed nations mainly because of a continuing influx of young immigrants. Nevertheless, it still reaches 28 per cent by 2030. Germany and Italy become the oldest nations on Earth with ratios of over 35 per cent. This is due to their having the slowest population growth rates in the world at present.

From this one critical demographic trend, various changes in societies are already surfacing. The biggest earthquake is that the governments of rich nations, having built up the welfare state in the twentieth century, are now having to forsake that role because they simply can't afford the burden of being nanny any longer. Ideology simply doesn't come into it. Elderly people are therefore going to have to work till later in life. While they are working, they will have to save more money for their retirement. In addition, they may be obliged to contribute greater sums to pension and medical aid schemes.

Secondly, elderly people crave security. Since they are due to make up an increasing percentage of the electorate, they will vote in governments who feature law and order at the top of their agenda.

Thirdly, on a more general note, older people may not be wiser, but they are more conservative. They will put greater pressure on governments to balance their budgets and cut down on public debt. They will demand that central banks use monetary policy to do nothing else but stabilise prices. They don't want to see their pensions eroded by inflation. They will want welfare to become workfare which links state benefits to a requirement to work. Thus, hand-outs would be restricted to the deserving (as opposed to the undeserving) poor.

The fourth change concerns the market. We have spent half a century catering for teenagers and baby boomers. That's where the pace has been set in the market. But now we're into the geriatric boom. It is already opening up vast opportunities for entrepreneurs in terms of walled retirement villages and the development of medical equipment and pharmaceutical drugs to overcome the common afflictions associated with advancing age. Of course, at a time when the state is set to diminish benefits for the elderly, medical products will need to be cost-effective to be successful.

1.3 HIGHER SAVINGS

As the world's population gets older, there will also be more middle-aged people. *Chart 15* indicates the percentage change in this important age cohort (45 to 54) in various countries between 1995 and 2010. The middle-aged constitute the high savers in society

MORE HIGH SAVERS
1995-2010: Projected change in the 45-54 age group as a percentage of the total population

US	+3,1	Hong Kong	+6,4
Canada	+2,6	Malaysia	+3,7
Germany	+1,7	Singapore	+6,1
France	+1,7	Thailand	+3,9
UK	+1,8	Korea	+4,6
Italy	+1,6	India	+2,8
Japan	−3,5	Mexico	+3,4
Sweden	−1,2	Argentina	+0,5
Switzerland	−1,0	Brazil	+3,5
		Venezuela	+3,1

Chart 15 *(Barclays de Zoete Wedd Securities Ltd., "Strategy 2000")*

inasmuch as they are too old to be spendthrift youths and too young to be spending all their money on staying alive. From an economic point of view, those countries which are due to have significant increases in this segment of the population are very favourably placed. The reason for this is the classical economic equation, "savings equals investment". When a country has a large domestic pool of savings, it has that much more money to satisfy the demand for new investment in plant and machinery. Hence, real interest rates are lower.

On the left-hand side of *Chart 15*, the middle-aged trend augurs particularly well for the United States and Canada, whereas Japan, Sweden and Switzerland suffer a decrease. But the greatest beneficiaries of an improvement in savings due to more middle-agers are clearly going to be the Asian Tigers and the others listed on the right-hand side.

1.4 SHARES OF WORLD OUTPUT

Chart 16 demonstrates another important consequence of the changing demographics and the increasing prosperity of developing countries. The chart is based on the outputs of the three most

SHARES OF WORLD OUTPUT
Based on real PPP weights in 1987 dollars

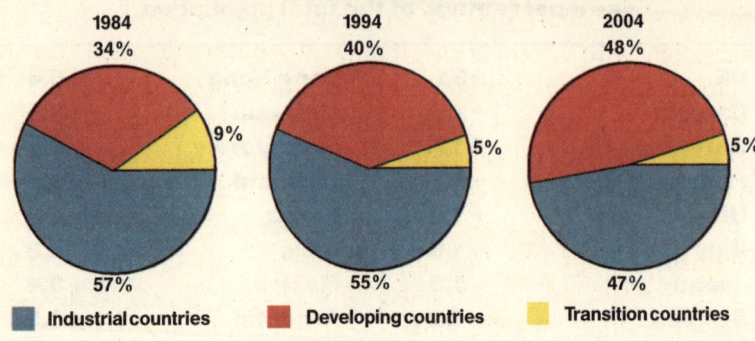

Chart 16 (AAC Research and Economic Services Dept., London)

important segments of the world measured in terms of purchasing power parity. In 1984, it made sense for successful exporters to target industrial countries as their markets because they represented 57 per cent of world output and therefore world income. Developing countries at the time constituted 34 per cent and the transition countries (Russia and Eastern Europe) were at 9 per cent. The position changed somewhat in 1994 when industrial countries' share of the pie declined slightly to 55 per cent, developing countries upped their share considerably to 40 per cent and the transition countries, due to the temporary collapse of their economies, went down to 5 per cent.

But, look at the position anticipated in 2004. For the first time developing countries will outstrip industrial countries in terms of world output while transition countries are expected to maintain their five per cent. This means that a successful exporter should in future target the whole world with his product rather than just the rich countries. India, for instance, now has 250 million middle-class people, which is the size of the American population. China, which also falls into the red segment of the pie, is building up a sizeable middle class too, and they all want to purchase the modern accoutrements of life. Entrepreneurs will make a feast of money in these markets if they exploit the right niches.

1.5 AIDS

At the time of our original study in 1986, we referred to AIDS as a wild card which could overturn demographic projections. However, along with violent crime, it now constitutes the biggest threat to South African society since the death of Apartheid. So you will forgive me if I dwell on the matter with a large selection of charts.

Chart 17 shows the current distribution of adults and children living with HIV/AIDS in mid-1996. Out of a global total of 22 million, 14 million are in Sub-Saharan Africa, 4,8 million in South and South-East Asia and 1,3 million in Latin America and the Caribbean. In all other parts of the globe, the figures are less than one million. For the moment, then, the epicentre of the HIV/AIDS scourge is Africa, although South and South-East Asia are expected to catch up as we move into the next century.

Given the African focus, our scenario team then looked at seroprevalence rates in various African countries. The figures shown in *Chart 18* relate to 1994 since more up-to-date statistics are generally not available. Nevertheless, the magnitude of the epidemic

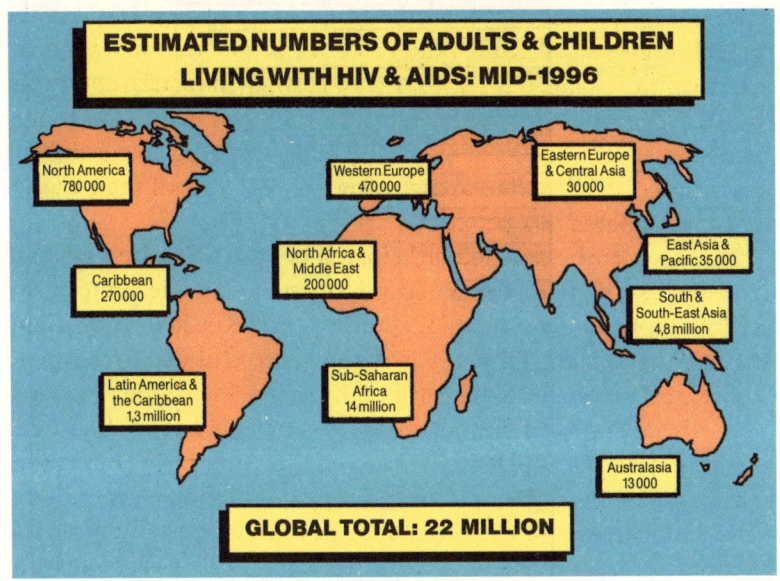

Chart 17 *(UN AIDS June '96)*

is plain to see. In the majority of countries, the urban centres (shown in red) are more badly affected than the rural areas (shown in blue). Rwanda's urban centres sit at 33 per cent with Malawi close behind. Then come Uganda, Zambia, Botswana, Swaziland and Zimbabwe which are all over 20 per cent. South Africa on the chart is shown at 7,5 per cent, but this figure has been recently revised by the Department of National Health to around 10 per cent.

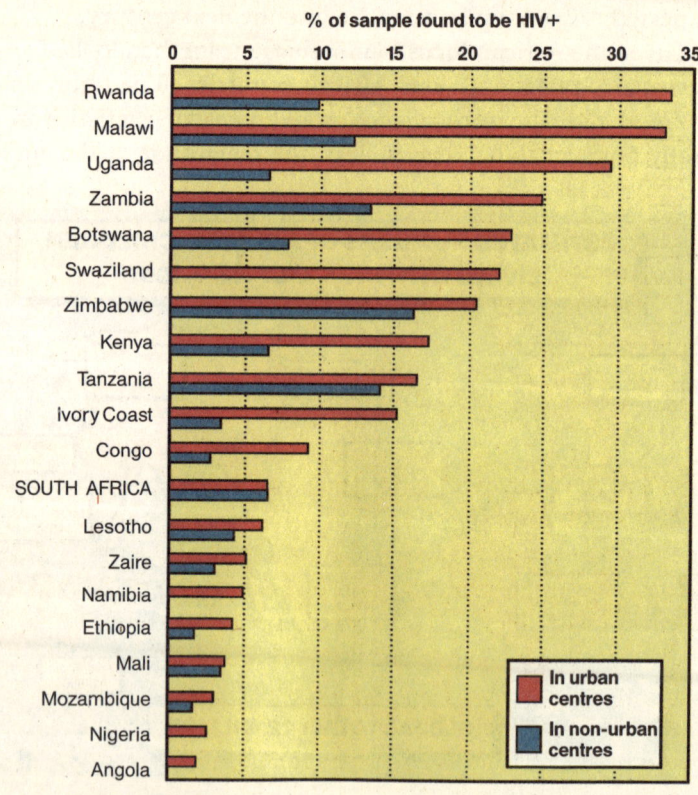

Chart 18 *(US Bureau of the Census)*

AFRICAN HIV-1 SEROPREVALENCE FOR LOW-RISK URBAN POPULATIONS

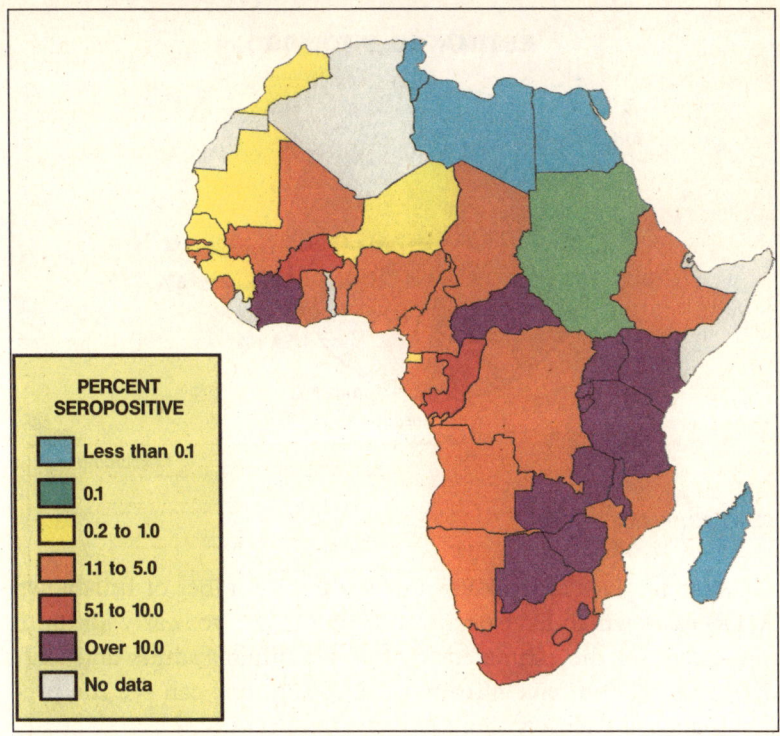

Chart 19 *(U.S. Bureau of the Census, Population Division, International Programs Center, HIV/AIDS Surveillance Database, Dec. 1994)*

Chart 19 is a map of Africa showing HIV distribution in colour coding. The countries coloured purple are over 10 per cent. On the extreme left is the Ivory Coast and in the centre the Central African Republic. On the right, one can see how HIV has spread down the east side of Africa (excluding Mozambique). Starting at the top we have Uganda and Kenya, then Burundi, Rwanda and Tanzania, followed by Zambia and Malawi, then Botswana and Zimbabwe and finally South Africa is just going purple too. Some people associate this downward spread of HIV from northeast to southwest with the main truck and lorry routes.

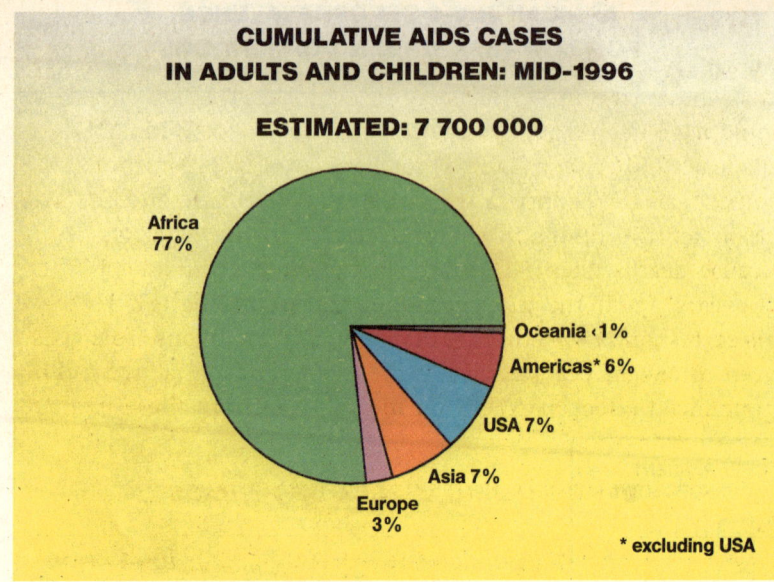

Chart 20 *(UNAIDS June '96)*

Chart 20 gives a breakdown of the total number of full-blown AIDS cases which have occurred from the late 70s/early 80s until mid-1996. Of the estimated total of 7,7 million adults and children, 5,8 million have already died. Again, one can see the predominance of Africa with a share of 77 per cent.

Chart 21 provides an estimate of the demographic effect of HIV/AIDS on population growth rates of the countries worst affected. You will notice that the epidemic is not projected to cause absolute decreases in population numbers between 1994 and 2010 other than in Thailand (where the population growth rate without AIDS is low anyway). For most of the rest, the two-and-a-half to three per cent per annum growth rates are reduced to between one and two per cent. Africa is not about to have vast empty areas which have been depopulated by AIDS. Nevertheless, the population in 2010, which without AIDS would have been 555 million collectively for all the countries listed, is estimated to be around 480 million with the disease.

Chart 22 reviews the actual life expectancy calculated for various countries in 1994 and the anticipated life expectancies without and with AIDS in 2010. Here, the impact is astonishing. In Kenya, for example, the life expectancy in a "without AIDS" scenario would have risen from nearly 60 to just below 70. With AIDS, it falls to 40. Other than Zaire which has a low seroprevalence at the moment, all the countries shown fall to between 30 and 40. The reason for the dramatic effect of AIDS on life expectancies is because deaths from AIDS are concentrated in infants/children (0-4 years) and in the 30-45 year adult age group. In the latter case, this corresponds with the fact that new HIV infections are highest seven to eleven years earlier at the peak of sexual activity. The pronounced effect of AIDS on mortality rates in these two age

DEMOGRAPHIC EFFECT OF HIV/AIDS

	Population Growth Rates, %/yr 1994-2010	
	without AIDS	with AIDS
Brazil	0,9	0,6
Burkina Faso	3,1	1,6
Burundi	3,0	1,9
Central African Republic	2,4	1,9
Congo	2,3	1,0
Ivory Coast	3,1	2,5
Haiti	2,1	1,3
Kenya	2,5	1,0
Malawi	3,2	1,6
Rwanda	3,5	1,7
Tanzania	3,0	1,5
Thailand	0,9	−0,8
Uganda	3,3	1,5
Zaire	3,3	2,9
Zambia	3,4	1,4
Zimbabwe	2,1	0,5
POPULATION in 2010	**555 m**	**480 m**

Chart 21 *(US Bureau of the Census, "World Population Profile: 1994")*

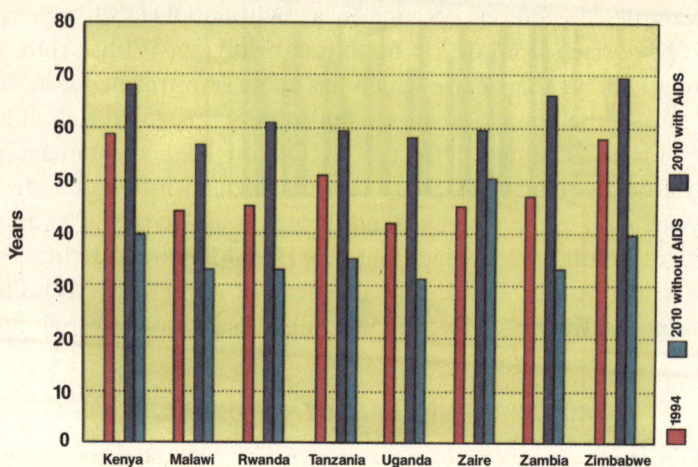

Chart 22 (US Bureau of Census, World Bank, Missen estimates for Rwanda, Zaire 1994)

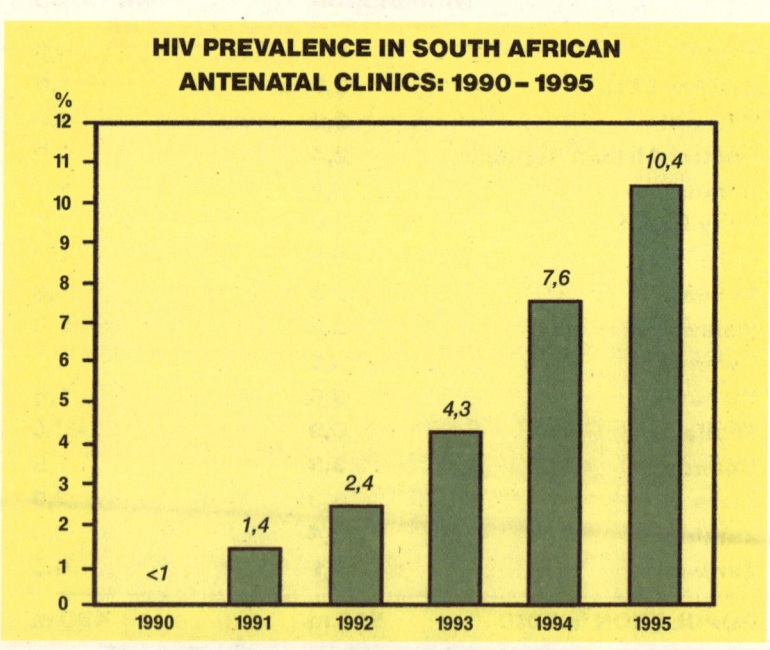

Chart 23 (Department of National Health – National Surveys of antenatal clinic attenders)

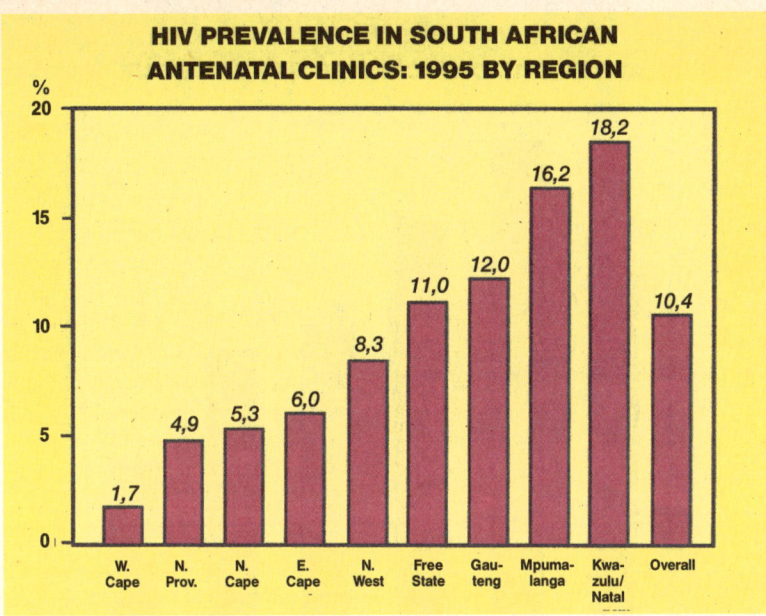

Chart 24 *(Department of National Health – Sixth National Survey of antenatal clinic attenders)*

cohorts drags down life expectancies considerably. With AIDS, life expectancy in South Africa is expected to decrease from its current level of 63,4 years to around 40 years in 2010. In contrast, the more muted effect of AIDS on birth rates (as demonstrated in *Chart 21*) is attributable to two facts: most adult AIDS deaths occur after childbearing age and HIV prevalence is lower in the rural areas where birth rates are higher.

Turning to South Africa, *Chart 23* registers the growth in HIV prevalence among antenatal clinic attenders from 1990 to 1995. From being negligible, it was 10,4 per cent in 1995, which shows how rapidly the epidemic is spreading. The national rate among adults will probably be a little lower than this.

Chart 24 exposes the regional diversity in seroprevalence in 1995. It highlights the fact that KwaZulu-Natal leads the other provinces at 18,2 per cent, followed by Mpumalanga at 16,2 per cent, Gauteng at 12 per cent and the Free State at 11 per cent. The Western Cape is lowest at 1,7 per cent.

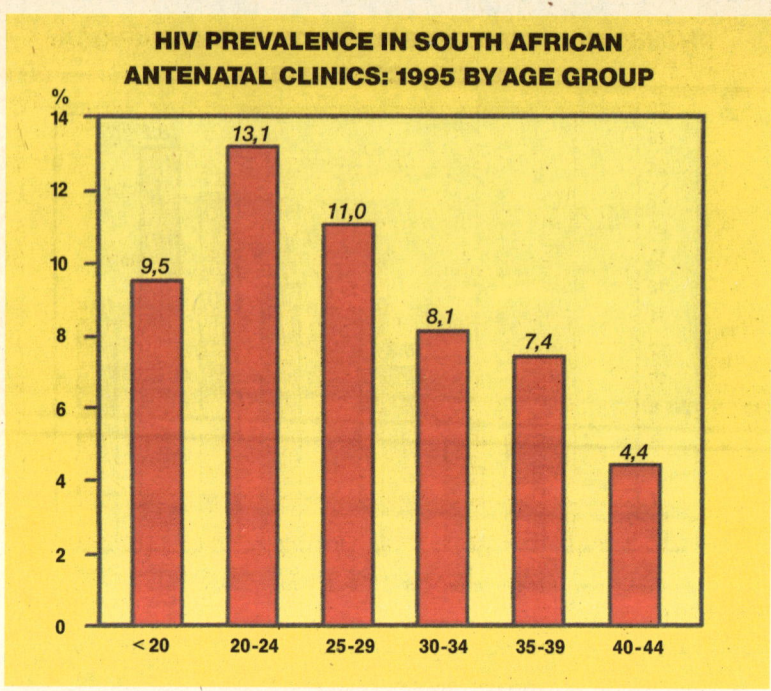

Chart 25 *(Department of National Health – Sixth National Survey of antenatal clinic attenders)*

Chart 25 analyses the distribution by age groups in 1995. The to 24 age cohort is highest at 13,1 per cent, followed by the 25- to 29-year-olds at 11 per cent. Significantly, the under-20 year-olds are at 9,5 per cent, which is made up mainly of infants and teenagers.

Chart 26 provides a projection of future HIV prevalence in South Africa. To be noted is the fact that infected females could be as high as 26 per cent in 2010 whereas males are estimated to be considerably lower at just below 18 per cent. The combined figure for both sexes in that year could be around 22 per cent.

Chart 27 depicts the number of reported AIDS cases in South Africa between 1982 and 1995. The exponential growth in AIDS is highly visible from this chart, though it must be said that there have only been 8 784 reported cases to date.

Chart 28 is a projection of the number of AIDS-sick people as

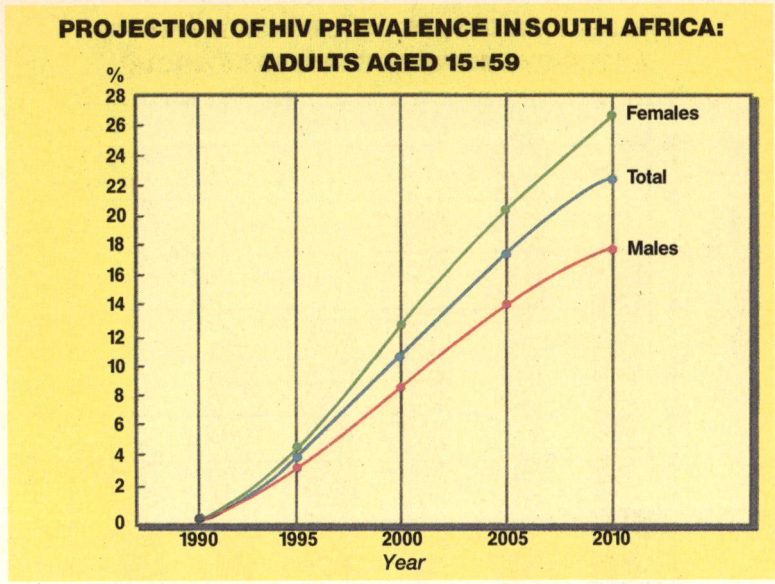

Chart 26 *(Doyle, June '93)*

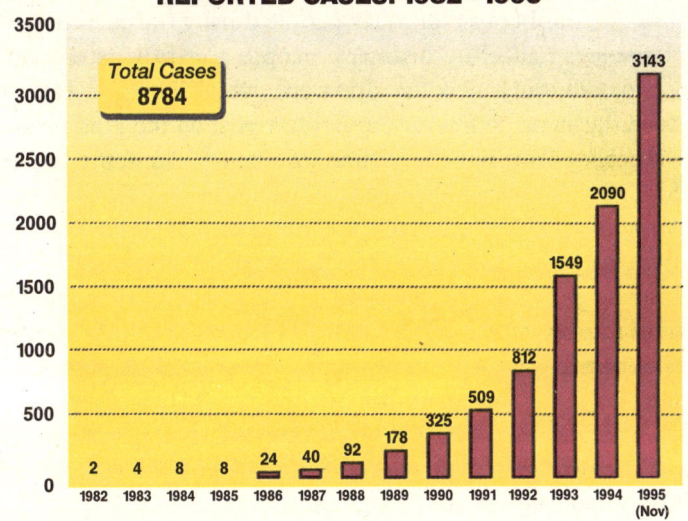

Chart 27 *(Department of National Health, Nov. '95)*

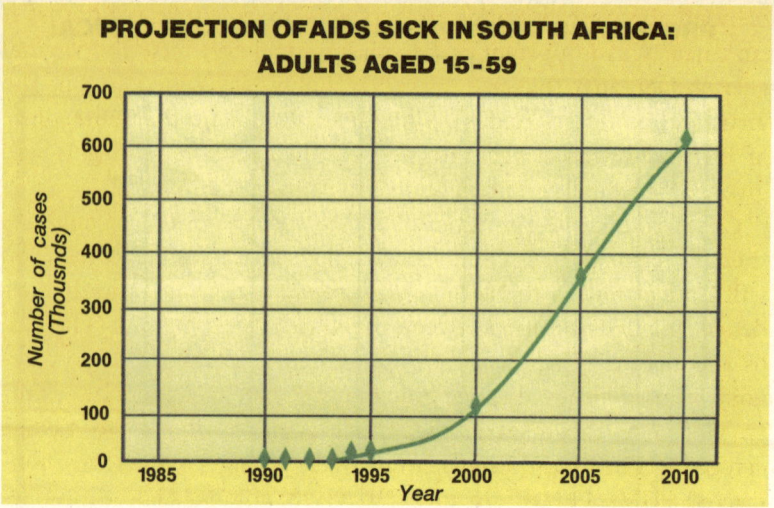

Chart 28 *(Doyle, June '93)*

South Africa moves into the new millennium. It could be as high as 600 000 in 2010. Essentially, this curve lags behind the curve shown in *Chart 26* by some ten years since that is the mean period it takes for a victim to progress from HIV to full-blown AIDS. The lethal nature of the epidemic can also be recognised from this chart, because the number of really sick people during the current decade is relatively small. For ordinary people the full extent of the epidemic will only become apparent after 2000. If HIV had followed the same course as the Ebola virus, which kills people in three weeks, perceptions and therefore behaviour regarding HIV would have changed much earlier. Tragically, by the time people are dying in sufficient numbers to alter sexual customs on a major scale, it may be too late. The HIV pool will be irreversibly high.

Chart 29 is highly relevant from the point of view of future progress to prevent the spread of HIV/AIDS. It shows the breakdown by mode of transmission for two periods: 1982 to 1989 and 1990 to 1994. Whereas in the earlier period transmission was mainly homosexual, it is now heterosexual. The probabilities of an HIV-positive man passing the virus to an HIV-negative woman are much higher in heterosexual sex than the other way around. For this reason, although the government should be commended for its campaigns to persuade men to use condoms, it isn't nearly as important as persuading women to use the vaginal gels and creams that are currently being developed to kill the virus (called microbicides). The latter should be the centrepiece of future education programmes. At least, creams and gels will give women the freedom of choice to protect themselves.

Chart 30 takes the number of AIDS cases to date and analyses them in terms of males and females in various age categories. You will notice that in the 0 to 4 age group, which has a high incidence, the distribution between the sexes is pretty even. The 5 to 9s and the 10 to 14s have a low incidence. In the 15 to 19 category, it is terribly sad to see how many female teenagers have fallen victim to the disease. The same goes for the 20 to 24 age category. They would have been much younger when they contracted HIV. The origin of HIV/AIDS among such young females has been ascribed to the fact that men, in seeking non-HIV partners, are selecting younger and younger women. It is a warning sign, that, while the press concentrate on *Sarafina 2*, extensive child abuse and school rape are going on underneath their

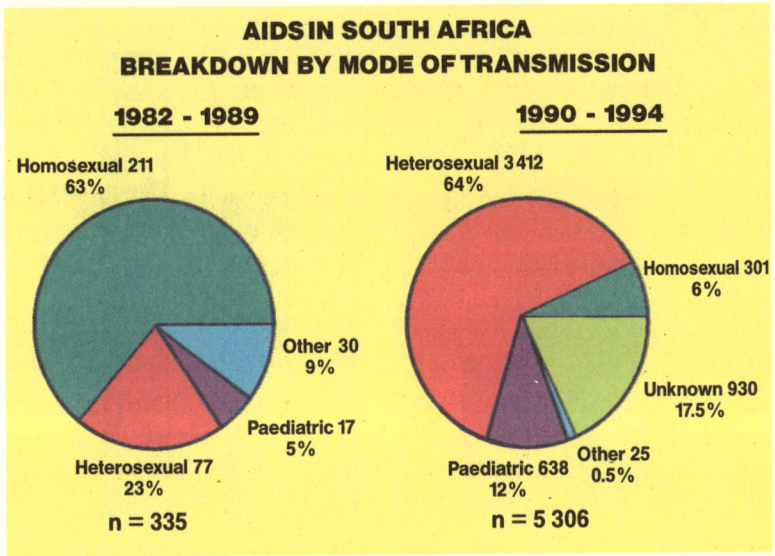

Chart 29 *(Department of National Health, Dec. '94)*

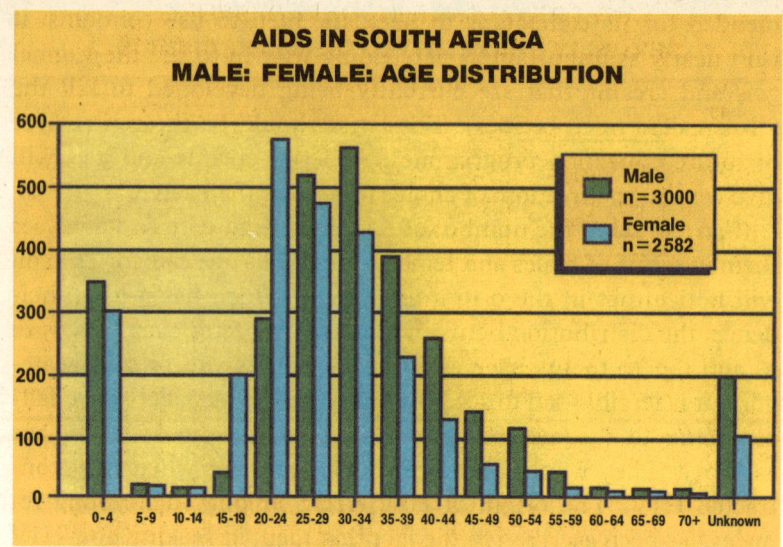

Chart 30 *(Department of National Health, Dec. '94)*

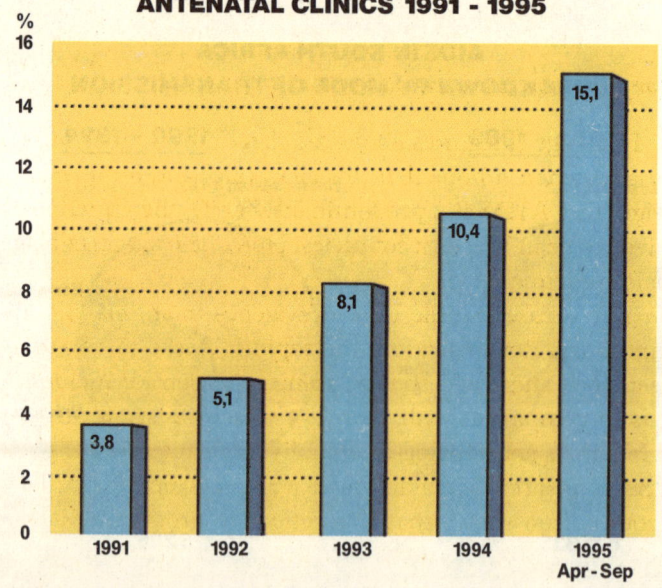

Chart 31 *(National Institute for Virology, Nov. '95)*

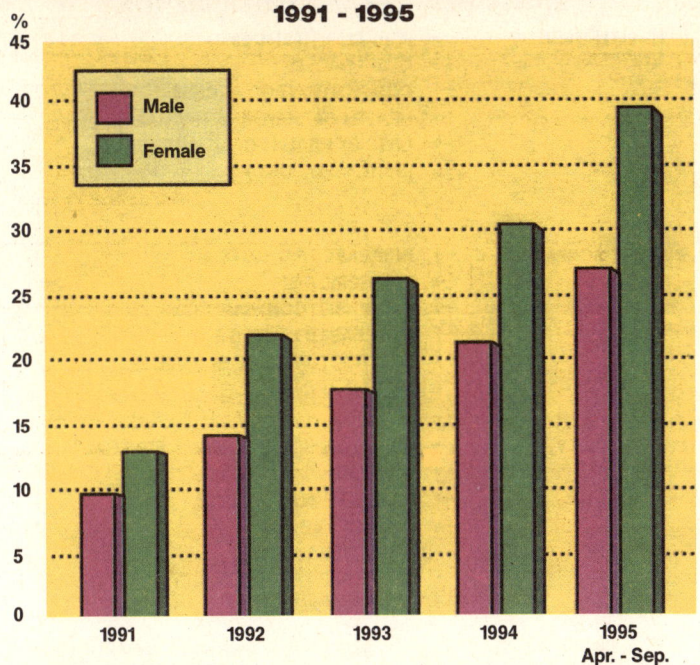

Chart 32 *(National Institute for Virology, Nov. '95)*

noses. In all age categories above 25, there are a higher number of men than women. I hope that this chart once and for all buries the paradigm that AIDS is a predominantly male phenomenon as it is perceived to be in Western countries. Here, below a certain age, it's a female epidemic.

Chart 31 focuses on the HIV prevalence in antenatal clinics in Johannesburg, demonstrating the rapid increase to 15,1 per cent between 1991 and 1995. But the primary reason for including this chart is to compare it with *Chart 32* which illustrates the prevalence in clinics specialising in sexually transmitted diseases. Note that the 1995 prevalence amongst women is nearly 40 per cent. The comparison shows that if an effective programme to reduce sexually transmitted diseases were instituted, this would automatically bring down the number of HIV transmissions.

IMPACT OF AIDS

HEALTH-CARE SYSTEMS	→ PARALLEL TB EPIDEMIC → OVERLOADED → COMPETITION FOR ACCESS → HEALTH-CARE WORKER MORALE → LOSS OF HEALTH-CARE WORKERS → INCREASED COSTS
BENEFIT SCHEMES	→ INCREASED PAY-OUTS → FINANCIAL RISK → INCREASED CONTRIBUTIONS → DECREASED BENEFITS → RESTRUCTURING OF SCHEMES
PRODUCTIVITY	→ ABSENTEEISM (SICKNESS & FUNERALS) → IR ISSUES → INCREASE IN ACCIDENTS → LOSS OF LABOUR → EMPLOYEE MORALE → DECREASED PRODUCTIVITY → INCREASED COSTS
SURROUNDING COMMUNITIES	→ INCREASED LOSS OF LIFE → DECREASE IN LIFE EXPECTANCY → LOSS OF BREADWINNERS → INCOME DIVERTED TO MEDICAL & FUNERAL COSTS → DECREASED SPENDING POWER → INCREASED POVERTY → BREAK-UP OF FAMILIES → INCREASE IN ORPHANS → MORE STREET CHILDREN / CRIME → INCREASED DROPOUT FROM SCHOOLS

Chart 33 (Crisp)

Chart 33 lists some of the more important outcomes from an AIDS epidemic in South Africa. Already we are seeing a parallel TB epidemic here. South Africa's average TB infection rate of

311 per 100 000 people is at least double that of Mozambique, more than three times that of Tanzania, and is well over the 250 per 100 000 found in other world TB hot spots. The Western and Eastern Cape figures eclipse the national average, with infection rates soaring to 490 and 430 per 100 000 respectively. As Dr Donald Enarson of the International Union Against TB and Lung Disease said: "I've investigated TB in more than 150 countries and South Africa's epidemic is the most frightening I've encountered."

Whilst the progress of TB in HIV-negative patients is sufficiently slow for it to be identified and cured, this is not the case in HIV-positive victims. TB can kill the latter in four months. Hence, in the United States, the nickname for TB and HIV is "Bonnie and Clyde". With AIDS triggering other opportunistic diseases besides TB, the hospitals in South Africa are going to be overloaded. This in turn is going to create competition for the facilities between AIDS victims and the victims of all other diseases. Health-care workers' morale will decline further as they have to work even longer hours. Some, especially those involved in invasive surgery, may catch HIV. This could lead to a general exodus overseas.

On account of the long stay in hospital which many AIDS victims will be forced to have, health costs could go up astronomically. Benefit schemes risk higher pay-outs and are therefore already putting caps on claims in respect of AIDS. The problem here is that many victims die of an opportunistic disease rather than AIDS per se and it will be impossible for medical aid scheme administrators to keep an accurate record of the primary cause of sickness and death of each patient. Equally, the ethical question is certain to be raised as to why costs associated with AIDS should be singled out for limitation, whereas costly operations associated with injuries sustained in accidents for which the victim is responsible are not. Road accidents are an obvious case.

Profitability of companies could well decline because of absenteeism associated with sickness and attendance at funerals. Greater fatigue as victims make the transition from HIV to AIDS could increase the number of accidents. Because of the loss of labour, employers will have to hire more than the requisite number of apprentices in the knowledge that some of them will die during the training programme.

The effect on surrounding communities will be dramatic. Many breadwinners will die and family income will be diverted to medical and funeral costs. The social welfare net will be stretched to the limit by the break-up of families, the increase in orphans and the number of street children and dropouts from schools. This chart has a predetermined quality about it. It is like the monsoon months in India. You know when it rains heavily upstream in the Ganges that the plains below are going to flood.

Against this utterly bleak background lies a small ray of hope. *Chart 34* illustrates the life cycle of HIV in human cells and the potential targets of drug therapy. There are several intervention possibilities depicted on the right-hand side. Viruses like HIV need cells within which to replicate themselves. HIV belongs to a rareish class of viruses known as retroviruses. Instead of DNA, the genes of a retrovirus are made up of its chemical cousin, RNA. HIV's RNA has nine genes, each a blueprint for one or more of the types of proteins needed to make new viruses. These proteins assist the virus in binding to and penetrating the cell. The particular proteins involved in HIV locking on to a human T-cell (imagine two space modules docking in orbit) are gp120 on the HIV side and CD4 and fusin as receptors on the other side. Once inside the cell, HIV persuades that cell to manufacture new proteins and new RNA using the genetic blueprints of HIV's RNA. An essential part of HIV's replication cycle is that it has to copy its RNA into DNA in order for the door into the host cell's nucleus to be opened. There the copied DNA integrates easily into the company of the host's genes and by manipulating the proceedings of the nucleus causes the cell to churn out new HIV. The process of copying RNA into DNA is called "reverse transcription".

The aim of anti-HIV drugs is to jam a specific step in the replication cycle. Up till a few months ago, the two drugs AZT and 3TC were the front-line defence. Like a tag team in a wrestling ring, they were used to stop the specific step of reverse transcription as shown in the chart. They won the first few bouts but inevitably, as their HIV opponent gained in experience and changed

LIFE CYCLE OF HIV IN THE HUMAN CELL AND POTENTIAL TARGETS OF DRUG THERAPY

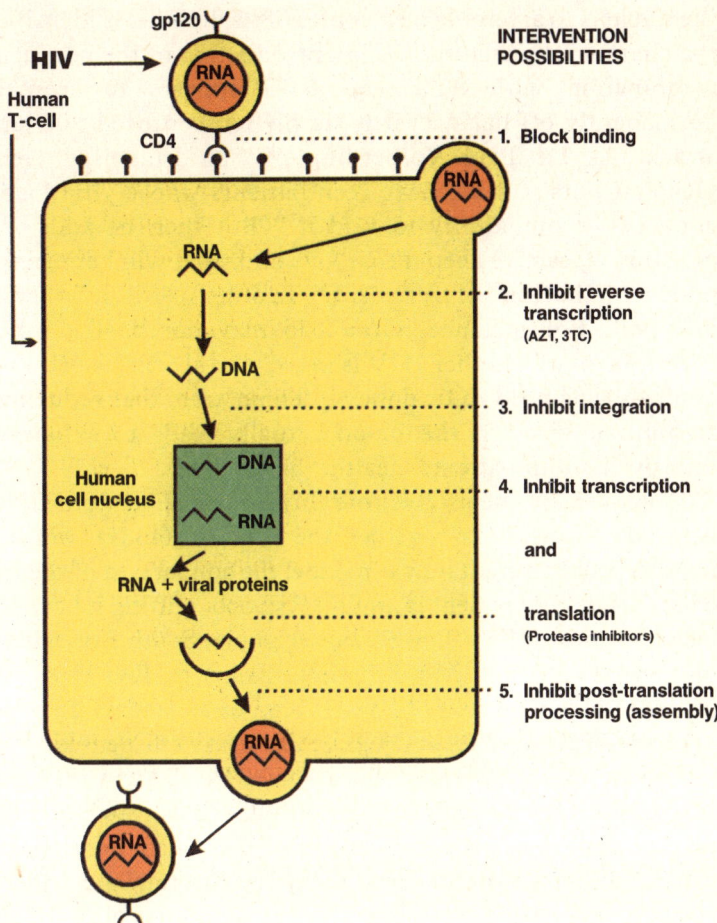

Chart 34 (Missen)

tactics, they lost the later bouts and finally the contest. The patient died.

But now a new class of drug has joined the attack. It is called a "protease inhibitor". Three products have been developed – Saquinavir from Hoffman-La Roche, Ritonavir from Abbott and Indinavir from Merck. A protease inhibitor interferes in a later part of the replication cycle – just when HIV is exiting from the nucleus to assemble new copies of itself. This is identified in the chart as "translation". The introduction of the new drug in combination with AZT and 3TC appears to keep HIV permanently off balance: it is simply too confused to counterattack. As Dr Paul Volberding of San Francisco General Hospital puts it: "We have seen patients whose viral load has gone below our ability to find it." But then he adds: "The question is, can we keep it that low, and what will happen to the body with that kind of treatment?" In other words, it's very early days yet. For instance, viral load may not be the ultimate determinant of whether HIV is present or absent. A great many clinical trials need to be done to demonstrate that reducing the amount of virus in the blood actually leads to a long-term improvement in patients' health.

Moreover, by themselves, the three medications can cause severe side effects; taken together, the position could be worse. But the real problem right now is money: the annual cost of the three-drug cocktail per patient is around R50 000, putting it beyond the means of most HIV sufferers. For example, South Africa has two million HIV victims. Multiply that number by R50 000 and you have a total annual sum of R100 billion or more than 20 per cent of our GDP, should these drugs be universally dispensed.

This raises an important ethical issue. We all know that, generally speaking, rich people in the world have access to better medical care than poor people. Even where good state hospitals exist, private clinics can outperform them because they are under less pressure and have more money. Yet an abiding goal of the twentieth century has been to give people as long a life as possible irrespective of financial means. We accept that a richer person can have a better car or a better house, but there's something less acceptable about the rich being able to purchase more years of life. If additional tests demonstrate the efficacy of the new cocktail to the extent that it either becomes a chronic medication or – dare one say it – a cure, it's going to be mighty tough on South Africa unless the drug companies lower their prices.

One final word about AZT. It can to a large extent prevent the transmission of HIV from mother to child. By giving an HIV-positive woman AZT at the end of her pregnancy, and during delivery, and then giving it to the baby afterwards, the risks of transmission fall precipitately. Take note, South Africa.

1.6 PLAGUES IN GENERAL

Before leaving demography and diseases, our overseas scenario team latched on to one other anxiety felt by Western doctors: the rise in potential for plagues generally. *Chart 35* shows the reasons. Going clockwise from the top left, we now have more international travel and migration than before to spread diseases. Marginalised people in the underclass of society do not look after their health. Urbanisation provides alarming potential for an outbreak. Imagine what would happen in Mexico City or São Paulo if Ebola erupted there! The sharing of needles in drug use and multiple partners in sex are both vehicles for transmitting diseases. Over-prescribed

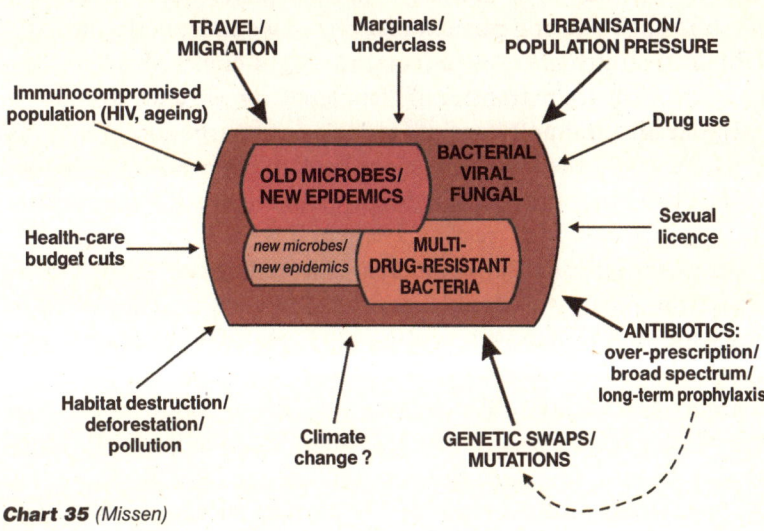

Chart 35 (Missen)

and poorly directed prescriptions of broad-based antibiotics, together with the use of antibiotics as prophylactics in developing countries, have induced genetic swaps and mutations in bacteria. They have now evolved into multi-drug resistant varieties.

The impact of possible global warming on bug proliferation has already been described. Habitat destruction and deforestation release previously confined viruses on populated areas. While all this is happening, governments are having to exercise greater stringency in determining their health-care budgets and populations are being immunocompromised by HIV and ageing.

A specific dread of the medical fraternity is clearly illustrated in *Chart 36*. Bacteria have an extraordinary facility to adapt genetically to external threats by transferring genes both within and between species. The enterococcus microbe, which is second on the list, has some strains which are now resistant to all 160 different antibiotics, including Vancomycin. Although this is not in itself cause for grave concern, because the enterococcus microbe only causes mild infections, it can only be a matter of time before the gene conferring Vancomycin resistance is passed on to the much more lethal staphylococcus aureus, the second last microbe listed in the chart. This will be a major catastrophe. Before the advent of penicillin in the early 1940s, staphylococcus aureus was often fatal by causing pneumonia, pus in wounds, boils, etc. Certain of its strains are now resistant to all but one antibiotic – Vancomycin. Thus, the transfer of Vancomycin resistance would give these strains immunity against today's entire armoury of antibiotics. We would then wind the clock back to the pre-penicillin era.

The two other microbes highlighted in red are TB and malaria. The estimated cost of treating a case of TB, including drugs, procedures and hospitalisation, increases from $12 000 in the United States for a drug-susceptible strain to $180 000 for a multi-drug-resistant strain. It also increases the odds of infectious disease outbreaks in hospitals.

Chart 37 indicates the global trend in TB in the nineteenth and twentieth centuries. After the dip following the discovery of the first TB drug in 1945, the number of annual TB deaths has climbed again to three million. The upturn prompted the World

AN EPIDEMIC OF RESISTANCE
TOP 10 COMMON DRUG-RESISTANT MICROBES

MICROBE	DISEASES CAUSED	DRUGS COMMONLY RESISTED
Enterobacteriaceae	bacteremia, pneumonia, urinary tract/ surgical wound infections	Aminoglycosides, Beta-Lactam antibiotics, Chloramphenicol, Trimethoprim
Enterococcus	bacteremia, urinary tract/ surgical wound infections	Aminoglycosides, Beta-Lactams, Erythromycin, Vancomycin
Haemophilus influenzae	epiglotitis, meningitis, otitis media, pneumonia, sinusitis	Beta-Lactams, Chloramphenicol, Tetracycline, Trimethoprim
Mycobacterium tuberculosis	tuberculosis	Aminoglycosides, Ethambutol, Isoniazid, Pyrazinamide, Rifampicin
Neisseria gonorrhoeae	gonorrhea	Beta-Lactams, Spectinomycin, Tetracycline
Plasmodium falciparum	malaria	Chloroquine
Pseudomonas aeruginosa	bacteremia, pneumonia, urinary tract infections	Aminoglycosides, Beta-Lactams, Chloramphenicol, Tetracycline
Shigella dysenteriae	severe diarrhoea	Ampicillin, Trimethoprim-Sulfamethoxazole, Chloramphenicol, Tetracycline
Staphylococcus aureus	bacteremia, pneumonia, surgical wound infections	Chloramphenicol, Ciprofloxacin, Clindamycin, Erythromycin, Beta-Lactams, Rifampicin, Tetracycline, Trimethoprim
Streptococcus pneumoniae	meningitis, pneumonia	Aminoglycosides, Chloramphenicol, Erythromycin, Penicillin

Chart 36 *(Science, Aug. 1992)*

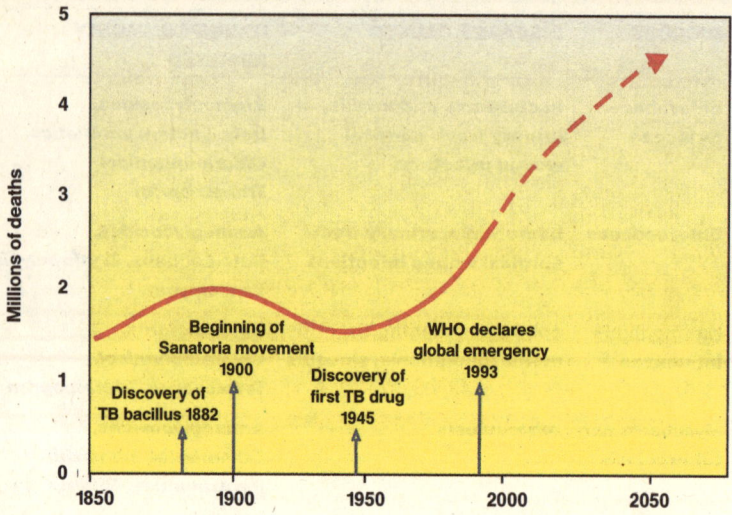

Chart 37 (World Health Organisation: Global Tuberculosis Programme estimates)

Health Organisation to declare a global TB emergency in 1993. In regard to malaria, northern KwaZulu-Natal has been on the receiving end of multi-drug-resistant strains leading to a surge in deaths this year. This could have a more adverse effect on tourism than AIDS. As one doctor put it: "We may be able to clobber the new strains with a new generation of antibiotics that are currently being developed, but one gets the distinct impression that the bugs are catching up with us."

The idea of a plague may sound outlandish as we end the twentieth century. However, just remember that in 1918/19 influenza killed 21,6 million people, more than twice the death toll of combatants in the First World War (9,7 million).

In a different context, one must add that the loss of genetic diversity in the plant and animal kingdom as farmers specialise more and more on only the successful strains and breeds is also worrying. The trend could render these two areas vulnerable not only to pests and plagues, but also to rapid changes in habitat associated with global warming. More than 90 per cent of the world's food is derived from fewer than twenty species of plants.

2 TECHNOLOGY

The second "rule of the game" over the next twenty years revolves around technological developments. Before we look ahead though, let's return to the past.

2.1 KONDRATIEFF CYCLES

Chart 38 summarises the long-wave cycles in the global economy since 1789. These were named Kondratieff waves after the Russian economist who first drew attention to them. The fascinating feature

LONG-WAVE CYCLES IN THE AGE OF INDUSTRIALISATION 1789-2045

	Period of expansion	Years duration	Period of adjustment	Years duration	Cycle duration	Expansion catalyst	Adjustment catalyst
KONDRATIEFF 1	1789-1814	26	1815-1847	33	59	Industrial & French Revolutions	Post-Napoleonic War recession
KONDRATIEFF 2	1848-1872	25	1873-1896	24	49	Central European revolutions	European & US financial panics/ banking crisis
KONDRATIEFF 3	1897-1920	24	1921-1947	27	51	Foreign investment boom. Trade liberalisation	Post-War reparations. German financial crisis
KONDRATTIEFF 4	1948-1973	26	1974-1994	21	47	Bretton Woods, Marshall Plan, Colonial independence	Bretton Woods collapse. OPEC oil crisis
KONDRATIEFF 5	1995-2020	26	2021-2045	25	51	End of Communism, Third World industrialisation	Global environmental crisis?

Chart 38 (Cass Research Associates)

of this chart is that the periods of the four economic upswings since 1789 have varied between 24 and 26 years. The first was triggered by the Industrial and French Revolutions; the second by the Central European Revolutions; and the third by booming foreign investment and trade liberalisation in the Edwardian era. People forget that Britain had one-third of its capital stock invested abroad in 1914 and was open to as much trade as it is now. The fourth upswing took place after the Second World War, partially as a result of American generosity in implementing the Marshall Plan to uplift Germany and partially due to the currency stability provided for years by the Bretton Woods agreement.

The periods of adjustment (or busts) that were interspersed between the booms are also listed, together with the reasons that precipitated them, in the last column. Their range of duration is slightly broader. Notably, the third contraction was ushered in by the world's excessive demands for reparations from Germany after the First World War. It included the Wall Street crash of 1929, together with the Great Depression of the 1930s caused by the Smoot-Hawley Act passed in America to protect domestic industry against foreign imports. The fourth contraction was precipitated by the oil price shocks during the 1970s. Overall, the average length of the four Kondratieff cycles to date is a shade over half a century.

On the basis of these cycles, we have just entered the upswing of the fifth Kondratieff wave, which should last from 1996 to 2020 and whose catalyst is the end of communism and the industrialisation of the Third World. The boom could be brought to an end by a global environmental crisis in 2021. However, that lies beyond our scenario period!

Before you think that I've entered the world of statistical sorcery, let me provide some hard physical backing to the Kondratieff waves. *Chart 39* depicts the advances in technology that have taken place since 1870. Intense periods of innovation which lead to major new waves have occurred at roughly thirty-year intervals. The nexus is therefore simple. When major new technologies are discovered, the rapid expansion of their applications leads to an economic boom. The world then has a breathing

THE DIFFUSION OF TECHNOLOGICAL WAVES

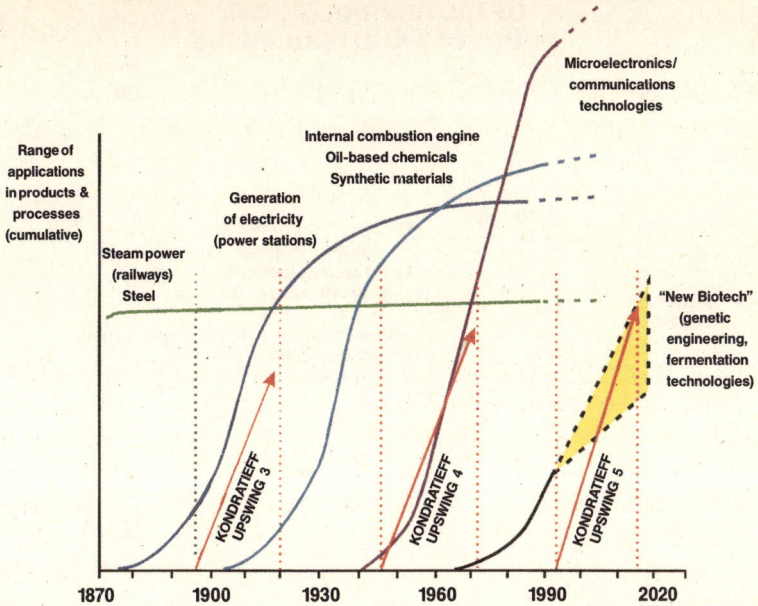

Chart 39 *(Adapted from Freeman, "Biotechnology, Economic and Wider Impacts", Paris, OECD '89)*

period or recession after the technology has reached saturation point.

In 1870 – the starting point of the chart – steam power, railways and steel were already used in a fairly wide range of applications. Then along came power stations and electricity which gave momentum to the third Kondratieff upswing that began in 1897. After that cars, plastics and early computers provided the launch pad for the fourth Kondratieff upswing.

The fifth one, that we are now in, was initiated by an even wider range of applications being discovered for microelectronics, particularly in the area of communication. Notice that each successive technology has had a more pervasive range of applications, with microelectronics outshining the rest by far. Furthermore, the latter part of the current upswing could be boosted by biotechnology, the latest wave.

So far biotechnology has been more a case of "bio-hype". For-

59

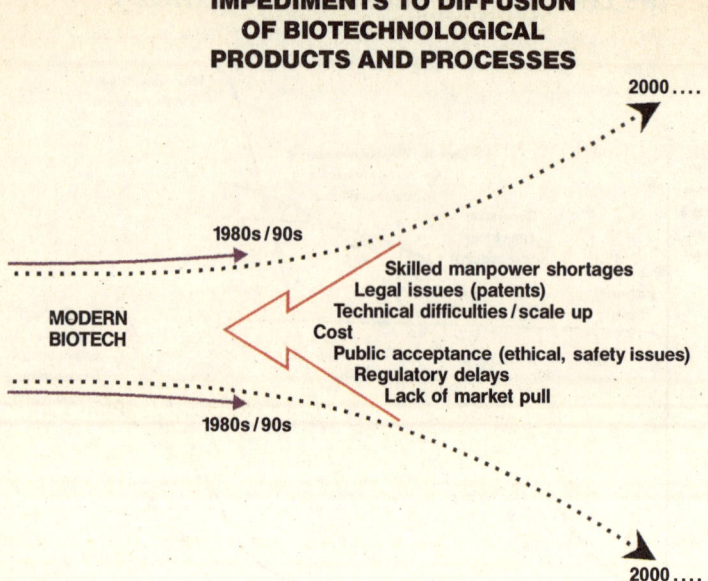

Chart 40 (Missen)

tunes have been lost in companies with promising innovations in this area, but which have come to nothing commercially. *Chart 40* explains why biotechnology has been so slow in taking off. Not only are there legal issues and regulatory delays (authorities are queasy about letting new animals or plants loose on this Earth), but the public have not yet accepted genetically engineered products. For example, a new tomato called "flavr-savr" has been on the market for some time. It has been genetically altered to prevent the production of an enzyme which leads to ripening/softening. Unfortunately, the public are still suspicious that such a tomato will modify their guts!

The field in which biotechnology has so far had most success is the manufacture of new biotechnologically derived drugs. You take the DNA chain of an existing living thing like a bacterium, yeast or even an animal or plant, sever it by using enzymes, insert a new gene, splice it together again and create a living factory capable of producing proteins which naturally occur in human bodies, but in minute quantities. The protein product can then be used as a pharmaceutical in its own right, as illustrated in *Chart 41*. Three of the twenty top-selling drugs in 1994 were genetically engineered in this fashion. Biotech-derived drugs now account for 5 per cent of world prescription drug sales.

2.2 LOCK-IN VERSUS PERPETUAL TRANSITION

Another perspective on the impact of future technologies on

ESTIMATED WORLD SALES OF BIOTECH-DERIVED DRUGS IN 1994

DRUG/BRAND	USE	SALES $'000	PLACE IN TOP 20
erythropoietin ("Epogen")	anaemia/renal failure	2 200	#4
insulin ("Humulin")	diabetes	1 450	#9
growth hormone ("Protropin")	growth disorders	1 100	#19
G-CSF ("Neupogen")	leukaemia	1 000	-
hepatitis B vaccine ("Energix")	hepatitis B	900	-
a-interferon ("Roferon")	various	900	#20 (1993)
factor VIII ("Humafac")	haemophilia	450	-
t-PA ("Activase")	heart attacks	320	-
other interferons, etc.	various	350	-
TOTAL		8 700 = 5% of world prescription drug sales	

Chart 41 (Missen)

industry has been provided by the Global Business Network, a company based in California headed by Peter Schwartz. He used to be head of the scenario function at Royal Dutch Shell and published one of the classic books on scenario thinking called *The Art of the Long View*. The GBN draws a critical distinction between industries which are in a state of "lock-in" and those which are in "perpetual transition". Chart 42 illustrates the difference.

A lock-in industry is one where you can make plenty of money out of a particular technological standard because it lasts for a long time. For several centuries the people who produced saddles, ran stables and manufactured stage coaches all made respectable profits. But then horses were superseded by cars. Other than recreation and racing, all businesses associated with horses evaporated. We now have entire communities and large business networks devoted to the motor industry. Moreover, it is difficult to foresee anything that could replace the car in its present form as a means of flexible transport on land. The internal combustion engine could be replaced in time by the electric motor or some form of hybrid engine. If this became a new lock-in standard, the oil industry would certainly feel the pinch.

In the same way, the recording business has seen three lock-in

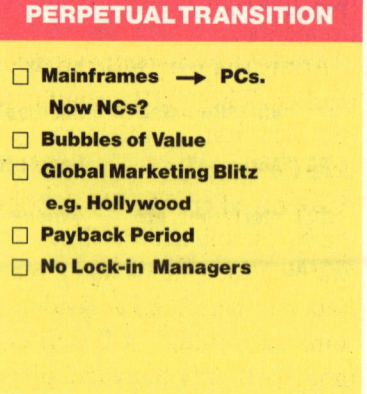

TECHNOLOGY SCENARIOS – A VIEW FROM CALIFORNIA

LOCK-IN	PERPETUAL TRANSITION
Substitution	☐ Mainframes ➝ PCs.
☐ Horses ➝ Cars	☐ Now NCs?
☐ 78s ➝ LPs & 45s	☐ Bubbles of Value
➝ CDs & Cassettes	☐ Global Marketing Blitz
☐ VHS vs Betamax	e.g. Hollywood
	☐ Payback Period
Parallel	☐ No Lock-in Managers
☐ Trains, Cars, Boats & Planes	
☐ Radio, TV, Videos & Movies	
☐ Paper & Internet?	

Chart 42 (Global Business Network)

periods this century. The 78s had their heyday in the 1920s, 30s and 40s. They were succeeded by LPs and 45s from the late 1940s to the early 1990s, which in turn were replaced by CDs and cassettes which are the recording standard today. The risk you take in a lock-in industry is to finance a plant to produce something which is about to be made obsolete by a shift in the standard. For example, it would not have been smart to construct an LP factory in the early 1990s. The Japanese, furthermore, discovered at great cost that you have to be extra careful in choosing what the next lock-in standard will be. They invested $9 billion in developing analog-based HDTV (high definition television) and have lost the lot. They didn't even gain any learning from it.

Lock-in industries sometimes see a battle between two rival technologies before one is established as a worldwide standard. Such is the case with the VCR industry which for a time had two standards: VHS and Betamax. For those who have a dusty old Betamax in their attic, you can take comfort in one thing. The salesman was right: Betamax's technology was superior in both vision and sound (it is still used by professionals) and it did come first to the market. What established VHS as the standard was a seemingly irrelevant factor – the duration of an American game of football. The VHS manufacturers were informed by RCA in the mid-1970s that the main attraction for the average American consumer of owning a VCR was to tape a game played by his favourite American football team. This lasted three hours with advertisements.

At the time, both Betamax and VHS had two-hour tapes on the market. The VHS manufacturers dedicated some of their best technical staff to the task of designing a four-hour tape and they beat Betamax to the market by a few months. This short lead period proved crucial. By the time Betamax caught up, VHS had already established itself as the dominant VCR in the United States. Video shops had already started stocking more VHS than Betamax tapes. As an aside, this is a classic case where scenario thinking would have benefited Sony, the maker of Betamax, enormously. If only Sony had played the scenario of the need to match instantly their competitors' strategy rather than relying on superior quality, Betamax might have been the worldwide standard today, with VHS VCRs in the attic. Often the blip on your radar screen can turn out to be a missile aimed straight at your tail by a wily competitor. Beware!

Sometimes lock-in technologies can exist in parallel. Trains were not put out of business by cars. They changed their function to carry cargo, to move people quickly between cities and to act as a mass transportation system in urban areas. Aeroplanes did not completely replace boats. But the function of boats changed to the carrying of cargo and taking people in ferries and on holiday cruises. Everybody thought that radio would be eclipsed by television. But American radio stations are having one of their most profitable years in decades. People like listening to talk shows. Movies have not vanished because of television and videos as some people thought they would. Nowadays, some experts are prophesying the end of paper with the advent of the Internet. But, as Robert Maxwell, the late notorious newspaper publisher, once said: "You can't read a CD-ROM in the bath!" It is therefore critical as a manager in a lock-in industry to decide whether a new technology will replace your product or service completely or modify its usage. For example, one must ask that question of the new digital video disc that threatens the VCR because it has stereo sound and a cinema-quality picture.

A final point to make about the lock-in principle is that it applies equally to primary industries like mining or agriculture. It is not that a new consumer product to replace the old one is introduced – the commodity remains the same whether it's copper, nickel, aluminium, wool, cotton, wheat or cattle. The action happens on the production side. New technologies come along which lower the real cost of producing the commodity. Even though, therefore, the real price of most commodities has declined over the past hundred years, it has still been perfectly possible to make very decent returns because the real unit cost on the other side of the profit equation has fallen even faster. World-class mining companies and world-class farmers are where they are because they are the first to exploit the shift from one lock-in technology to another (and they may even be the inventors themselves).

The other camp that industries fall into these days is the one of perpetual transition. This is where new technologies are introduced so fast that product life cycles are measured in months rather than years. As one electronic engineer put it: "dog years"! With the codification and computerisation of knowledge and the use of computer-aided engineering and computer-aided draughting, the lead times from conceptualisation of a product through prototyping and testing to production have been compressed dramatically. Linkages between universities and industry have greatly increased in the search for generally applicable design rules. At the same time, costs have been reduced because you no longer have to reinvent the wheel. You just call up any part of the wheel on your terminal from a database somewhere in another part of the world. You may have to pay for the intellectual property rights, but the knowledge is instantly there. Moreover, computerisation allows you to test a new product like a car or an aeroplane under an incredible range of complex conditions which would be impossible to simulate in the real world. You can also look at an awesome range of product variants to optimise the one you have in mind.

IBM for years was in a lock-in business. Each generation of IBM's mainframes set the standard for the industry until IBM decided that there should be a new standard. But that all changed with personal computers (PCs), and suddenly the computer industry moved to perpetual transition. This is another outstanding example of where scenario thinking might have allowed "Big Blue" to retain its premier position. It is one thing to be knocked off the perch by a competitor's product – it is quite another thing to be torpedoed by a product that you invented yourself, because you were locked into an old paradigm. If IBM had played the scenario that the PC would one day be at the centre of the information industry, maybe it would have at an early stage evolved an entirely different strategy to market its PC.

PCs are in a state of perpetual transition. You bring the latest version home with the latest software and the latest microprocessing chip. Then within a few months your son is complaining that the new computer game that he has just bought goes too slowly on your machine and you must upgrade. Even the entire genus of PCs is under threat from NCs (network computers) which can download software directly off the Internet. Such boxes will be much cheaper to buy. They will do exactly what you want, when you want it, but no more – in contrast to the PC which for many is a ridiculously overengineered device. Even proprietary PC software programmes could be rendered obsolete by the Internet because of the ease with which programmes can be exchanged between users of the network.

So what you have is bubbles of value that you have to make money out of. You have got six months to make it and that's all. When you launch your product, you need a global marketing blitz. Hollywood does that with a new movie which has to be seen in every single cinema in the world before another one makes it look stale. Gone is the old marketing strategy of seeing whether a product works in your town; and if it does, then marketing it nation-wide; and if it works there too, then exporting it around the globe. You have to do everything at once. The people who are successful at exploiting bubbles of value reap unprecedented rewards. Netscape's Marc Andreeson, the technical whiz who developed the Navigator Web browser for the Internet, was suddenly worth $58 million after Netscape's initial public offering in August 1995.

Alan Brinkley, professor of history at Columbia University, puts the heady ascent of Andreeson into perspective: "I don't think there was ever a period when wealth was created so instantly through the market as it is today. Certainly there were many people who rose from modest wealth to vast riches over a lifetime at the turn of the century – specifically, those in railroads, steel, oil and the big, rapidly growing industries of the time. But it was nothing like the people today who are worth a few hundred thousand dollars one day and take their companies public the next and become billionaires." The wonders of modern communication permit any inventor of a "killer application" to join the get-incredibly-rich-quick crowd like Andreeson has. So what's next after the VCR, the Walkman and the cellular telephone? The hunt is on.

In a perpetual transition world, orthodox tools of financial evaluation are no longer appropriate. When any cash flows beyond six months are highly uncertain, what use are discounted cash flow yields, internal rates of return and present values based on financial projections over twenty years? The only thing that counts is the payback period, and it has to be very quick. Perpetual transition is a nightmare for many big companies because it doesn't allow for large projects with decades of positive cash flows which make a substantial difference to the bottom line. It is more a case of having lots of successful little projects, each with its own bubble of value. Nobody is safe, because the perpetual transition virus is likely to spread into many traditional industries.

Lastly, you cannot put lock-in managers in charge of perpetual transition businesses because they will simply go bust. Lock-in managers do not have the fleet-footedness to survive. Experience is a handicap because it is more difficult to unlearn received wisdom than to learn new truths.

Chart 43 shows the difference in performance between AT&T,

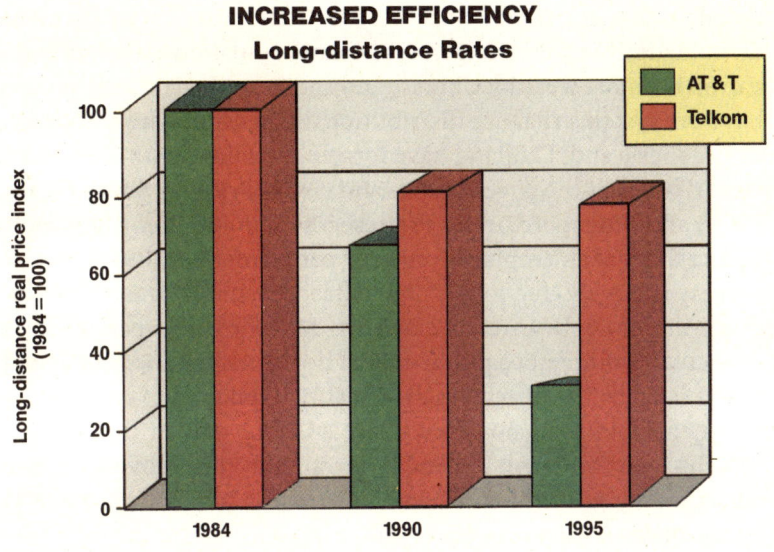

Chart 43 *(SA Foundation,"Growth for All")*

a private telephone company in America, and Telkom, a public company here, when faced with a world of perpetual transition. Their respective long-distance rates have been indexed at 100 in 1984. One can see that in the following eleven years AT&T reduced its real price of providing telecommunication services by 75 per cent compared to a reduction of 25 per cent by Telkom. AT&T took advantage of new technologies sooner, or even invented them. It surfed on each wave as it broke.

3 VALUES

Turning to the third "rule of the game", the important topic of values, our team discovered that in the realms of economic growth and public policy there really is something for everyone. An air of pragmatism reigns where each government selects policies that work for that particular nation.

3.1 SOMETHING FOR EVERYONE

Chart 44 indicates that in Japan and South Korea it works for governments to be fairly interventionist, whereas in Hong Kong and Thailand they stay out of the way. In Malaysia explicitly redistributional policies work because they bring social harmony through uplifting the indigenous Malay population and closing the gap on the more wealthy Chinese and Indians. Most other countries have tax systems that are distributionally neutral. The authorities in Indonesia and Thailand have forged close links with the private sector, whereas the governments and civil services of South Korea, Japan and Singapore prefer to preserve their autonomy. In South Korea there is an emphasis on large conglomerates, but Taiwan's success is largely due to its small entrepreneurial firms. Imitators must therefore beware of slavishly following the pattern of a particular country because it might not work for them and they might have got the direction of causality wrong.

Having said that, however, there are four golden threads that run through the Asian Tigers. They all have lean government as measured by governmental expenditure as a percentage of GDP. In most cases this ratio is around 20 per cent whereas in South Africa we stand at 31 per cent. This has been the century of the

ECONOMIC GROWTH & PUBLIC POLICY

Something for everyone

- Interventionist (Japan, South Korea)
- Non-interventionist (Hong Kong, Thailand)
- Explicitly redistributive policies (Malaysia)
- Distributionally neutral (most others)
- Clientelism (Indonesia, Thailand)
- Strong autonomous states (South Korea, Japan, Singapore)
- Emphasis on large conglomerates (South Korea)
- Emphasis on small entrepreneurial firms (Taiwan)

Four Golden Threads

* Lean government
* Highly supportive of business
* Outward looking for profitable niches
* Addicted to change

Chart 44 *(Sarel, Jacques)*

aggrandisement of the state. The UK's public spending rose from 12 per cent of GDP in 1913 to 40/50 per cent for most of the past three decades. The patterns in all other Western countries have been similar, but the Asian Tigers have so far avoided the trap. Lean, however, doesn't mean weak. The Asian Tigers have lean, but active government.

Secondly, governments of the Asian Tigers are highly supportive of business. For example, the intervention in Japan and South Korea is not of the "we're going to slap you on the wrists, you capitalist pigs" variety. Quite the reverse. The government acts as a coach trying to optimise conditions for business. All Asian Tigers realise that business is the number one activity and the government and civil service are there to support it.

Thirdly, the Asian Tigers are not trying to be all things to all people. They look very selectively for profitable niches in foreign markets which play to their strengths. They specialise in what they're good at. South Africa can take a leaf out of this book. Tourism has to be the best bet here, given our diversity of fauna and flora. By promoting bed-and-breakfast accommodation, lots of jobs can be created too.

Finally, Asian Tigers are addicted to change and are prepared to shed whole industries and grow new ones in their place if the global markets dictate this. If your per capita income is doubling every ten years, your society is going to be transformed very quickly.

3.2 POSTMODERNISM

Moving on to lifestyle values, we have entered an age of "postmodernism", as the title of *Chart 45* demonstrates. This is the view of a remarkable lady called Judie Lannon, who addressed our scenario workshop in September last year. The previous era of "modernism" lasted from the Industrial Revolution in the mid-eighteenth century to the 1980s. Modernism was based on mass production, class-based identity and collectivist philosophies. With the advent of the Internet and other communication technologies, together with the growth of small business, particularly in the services field, we have now moved to a more individualised culture. The level of affluence and the importance now laid upon individual rights have created an environment in which individuals

POSTMODERNISM

* **CONTINUOUS QUESTIONING OF CERTAINTIES**
* **AUTHORITY GAPS AND ETHICS GAPS**
* **FORCES SHAPING THE BUSINESS ENVIRONMENT**
    → information as the source of wealth creation
    → birth of global culture
    → left/right replaced by absolutism/pluralism
    → the Wizard of Oz revealed
* **COMPANIES THAT PEOPLE BELIEVE IN**

Chart 45 (Lannon)

are more free to transform themselves than at any other time in history. They have the space to "shop" for new meanings and a new personal identity.

Hence, we are now seeing the continuous questioning of certainties and experiencing an extreme fragmentation of the society that once seemed so coherent despite or maybe because of the two world wars. Ironically, fifty years of peace have placed unprecedented strains on the social fabric of the Western world.

Society has atomised. The power that has been decentralised to individuals will never be returned to the state. Like Humpty Dumpty, society as we have known it for the last 250 years will never be put back together again. The scientific law of entropy which says that a system left to itself will naturally wind down to ever greater levels of disorder applies in the social dimension as well. Hence, the idea that we are living in abnormal times is false, for it suggests that we might move back to normal times after a period of aberration; and the marketing and business practices that have flourished in normal times will work again. Not so. There may be economic cycles, but there is not about to be a cycle in social values. Although we are speaking principally here of the Western world, it is surprising how much the Western world acts as a pathfinder to the rest of the nations on Earth.

Readers who grew up in the 1950s, or the parents of younger readers of this book, will understand exactly what I mean. In the 1950s we had a narrow definition of family and gender roles and a sharp perception of social class. As a kid, one was accustomed to two parents, with perhaps one or two sisters or brothers. Mother stayed at home while father went out to work. If you did something wrong, you were disciplined. One quickly began to know who in society was superior or inferior to you in the sense of class. At school, a hierarchy existed where students accepted teachers as their superiors. After leaving school you knew that you could get a job in some large manufacturing concern and you would eventually marry and repeat the process of having children. At the time, religion still retained a pervasive and guiding moral influence and the neighbourhood was a community with norms and good neighbourliness. Politicians were respected. Nation states were regarded as permanent and governments had an unchallengeable authority over their citizens. You automatically paid your rates and taxes.

Now kids are surprised if they have a mother and a father to bring them up. More likely is that they never meet their father who, in any case, never supports them. Should they have two parents they almost expect both of them to be pursuing careers at the same time. If as infants they do something wrong, they expect counselling and reconciliation. When they go to school, they soon learn that teachers are their equals and can at any time be treated with disdain. If teachers go on strike or a go-slow or don't pitch up for afternoon sport, the kids shrug it off. After they leave school, they know that there is no certainty of a job and going on the dole is a nice alternative. If they're like their parents, they'll take a Prozac or Valium and chant "don't worry, be happy".

In other words, there are no guarantees about anything. So now we have authority gaps and ethics gaps. This may sound like a new version of the old generation gap, but it isn't. Certainly, the 1920s had F. Scott Fitzgerald and the 50s and 60s had rebels like James Dean, Marlon Brando and Elvis Presley and angry young men like John Osborne. But at least in those days there was a structure and an establishment to rebel against. Today there is no structure because everything is relative. Even the Ten Commandments are up for grabs. "Thou shalt not kill" has become "thou can kill under certain circumstances and let's negotiate the circumstances". Without absolute moral truths, the younger generation have no navigational aids. Without the wrath of an Old Testament God, they have no fear of retribution. Even Hell is no longer pictured as a place of eternal torment, a flaming pit full of demons and devils. Fire and brimstone have been replaced by a "state of nonbeing". Add to this the absence of authority and hierarchy in this world and you have no checks on youthful behaviour at all.

If you believe that I've gone over the top, take a good look at *Chart 46* which lists the top seven disciplinary problems in US schools in 1940 compared to 1990. The source was not a right-wing organisation like the John Birch Society, but the *Congres-*

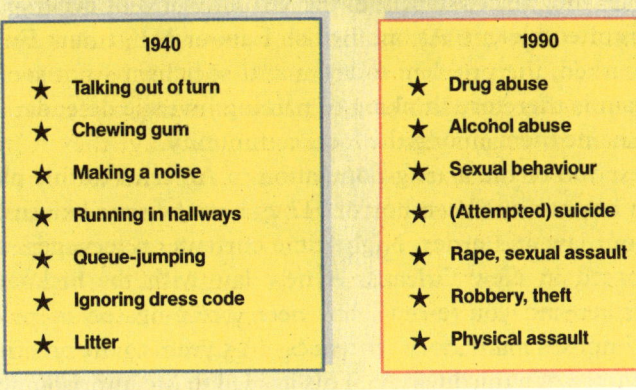

Chart 46 (*Congressional Quarterly*, Nov. '93)

sional Quarterly, November 1993. The list on the left consists of minor infractions whereas the list on the right is about major criminal activity. In no way can this be called progress. In fact, it represents serious moral retrogression. Across the Atlantic in Britain, teachers have had to resort to threats of striking en masse if disruptive pupils are not expelled. As one member of my audience asked – could the list possibly get worse in 50 years' time? The fastest growth in homicides in the US is taking place amongst youths aged between fourteen and seventeen. *Lord of the Flies* is no longer fiction. Moreover, this terrifying trend of violent, amoral, dead-eyed teenagers who show no remorse and no self-restraint is universal. It is not, as many people feel, confined to South Africa.

The causes of this amorality are probably manifold. The collapse of the family must rate at the top. A secondary reason I would trace to the "turn on! tune in! drop out!" fantasies embodied in the hippie culture of the 60s. The phrase, incidentally, is attributable to the late Timothy Leary who was the 60s icon of LSD and other mind-altering drugs (he died on 31 May 1996 and asked for his ashes to be shot into space). The hippie philosophy plus modern TV and video games have led to a generation of children growing up without social skills who believe the world is a dangerous place. Instead of developing real relationships with real people, they're constantly in the virtual world of cyberspace – which is often violent. As one British Labour MP, Frank Field, aptly remarked, the problem today is anti-socialism – not socialism. Britain is therefore thinking of naming juvenile defenders in order to shame them among the local community.

The reaction of the ageing population in America to this phenomenon has not just been horror. They have become extremely tough about law and order. Night-time curfews on teenagers are now enforced in New Orleans. A new law with the nickname "three-strikes-and-you're-out" has been promulgated in many states. It imposes mandatory sentences of 25 years to life on criminals convicted of a third felony. This has led to life imprisonment for a man who stole a slice of pizza and another who shoplifted three steaks – in both cases third offences. "Truth-in-sentencing" laws are also becoming fashionable. These require a criminal to serve at least 85 per cent of his sentence, whatever his conduct in jail. The purpose of prison has switched from rehabilitation to containment, i.e. keeping dangerous criminals out of society's way for as long as possible. All these measures are making jails a very big business in the US and are swelling the prison population. The latter could easily double from one to two million in the next four years, which would create an extra tax burden of $25 billion a year.

Despite the blizzard of new laws, regulations and codes of conduct which have been formulated by increasingly litigation-prone societies in the West, the authority gap stubbornly persists. Witness the growth of private militias, clans, vigilante groups, terrorist groups, religious cults, urban gangs and rural bandits. The power of the state has been drained away by such subnational organisations carving out empires of their own. The helplessness of a modern society in the face of fanatics who want to kill or maim innocent people through bombs is illustrated almost every day in the press. It is pretty safe to assume that the proportion of really evil people among mankind has remained constant throughout history. It certainly hasn't diminished. This means that, given the world's record population, they are far more numerous now. So we have two further records in the world: the highest number of evil people around with the least level of authority to control them. Add to this the fact that the world's population is increasingly clustered in cities and towns and therefore more susceptible to terrorist attacks and you realise that postmodernism can turn very ugly indeed.

3.3 FORCES SHAPING BUSINESS ENVIRONMENT

Returning to *Chart 45*, let us now look at the forces shaping the business environment. Information is the source of wealth creation. You need look no further than Bill Gates, who is worth $18 billion or over R80 billion. You have an individual who is forty years old, looks like John Denver and is worth more than the entire market capitalisation of the Anglo American Corporation. It is because he is chairman of the most successful company in the information field: Microsoft.

Equally, for companies not directly involved in the information business, the need to use state-of-the-art information technologies is paramount. Otherwise your competitors hear about and exploit revolutionary new ideas first. I have my own example of just how much the world is shifting in terms of information gathering. In order to tell the story of Betamax versus VHS in the earlier section on technology in this book, I asked our company library to give me as much information as they could on the development of the VCR. In the old days this would have meant the librarian blowing the dust off the only book on the shelves that had a reference to a VCR. Now she switches on the library's PC and starts surfing the Internet for information. In this case there was not much to be had from the site "Recording Technology History". So we accessed a private database which has every single article published in every single business journal since 1971. She fed in several key words: Sony, Matsushita, VHS, Betamax and VCR. There were several thousand references to each of the words, so she cross-referenced the five words and asked the data base how many articles contained all five words. The answer was

46. We then flipped through the abstracts of each article and finally came upon "Strategic Manoeuvring and Mass Market Dynamics: The Triumph of VHS over Beta", by Cusumano, Mylonadis and Rosenbloom in the *Business History Review*, Spring 1992. The abstract showed that we had hit the mother lode. There was a full copy available online and within thirty minutes of making the request the article had been e-mailed and printed out. Imagine that! We had flitted through all the business journals in the world since 1971 for this one article. It is why we now talk of the "information superhighway" and why Bill Gates declared that the Internet is as big a leap for mankind as the Gutenberg Press was in the fifteenth century.

We have the birth of global cultures. Many competing religions, value systems and lifestyles have always existed, but have not necessarily been widely known. They are now clearly visible via the Internet, global television networks as well as mass travel. This produces the kind of marketplace in which all manner of belief systems and lifestyles are offered for consumption. There was a picture on television the other day of an Israeli student with a can of Coca Cola in one hand and a rifle in the other wearing a "Grateful Dead" T-shirt. What a mixture of ideologies and fashion styles – an Israeli American Deadhead!

It is important to understand that this trend is not leading to a blander, more homogenous world. Cultures, though mixed, are still distinct. For this reason, some of the most successful global brands are highly nationalistic. If you buy a Coke, like the soldier did, you are in effect buying American youth in a bottle. If you're rich enough to afford a Rolls Royce, you're buying English heritage on wheels. Culture, as someone said, is the software of the mind. Different software packages are often incompatible, but can still communicate with one another if the right gateways are found.

The Left/Right debate is now dead with the collapse of the Soviet Union and other centrally planned economies. Anybody who calls himself a communist these days is merely a closet capitalist. This debate has been replaced by one between "absolutists" and "pluralists". An absolutist is a person who believes that his/her idea is more important than any other idea in the world. In order to get the world to revolve around the idea, he/she will get together with like-minded people to form single-issue lobby groups, societies or NGOs (non-governmental organisations). These can be very powerful because they are so focused. Absolutists come in many forms in areas such as feminism, political correctness, the environment and religion. In the last case, one usually calls such people fundamentalists, whether they are Islamic fundamentalists, born-again Christians or ultra-Orthodox Jews. They seek solace in sacred codes that offer metaphysical reassurance and detailed regulations of private behaviour. They want to get away from the uncertainties and moral relativism of modern society. They find peace in absolute authority.

Pluralists, on the other hand, believe that there is a little bit of good in everything. One should tolerate alternative views, compromise between them and muddle through. Life is about making an optimal balance. Frederik van Zyl Slabbert once made a very wise comment in a speech: "The hardest choices are not between good and bad, but between good and good, where pursuing one good alternative means less good in another direction." He's a pluralist!

Chart 47 explains the basis of pluralism: human wellbeing springs from a combination of environmental health that gives you clean skies, clean water and clean beaches; economic development that makes you richer; and quality of life that makes you better. All the Arts fall into the last category. In contrast, absolutists can be found in the outer reaches of these three circles. Deep greenies believe that only the environment matters and we should therefore ride bicycles and eat berries in order not to pollute it. This ignores economic development. Free-enterprise freaks on the other hand are obsessive about economic growth even if this causes an environmental bust. Zen-like intellectuals inhabit an abstract universe where materialism doesn't count and the only objective is quality of life – not in this world but the next.

Any dynamic society has its fair share of absolutists as well as pluralists. Sometimes it is right to be an absolutist and take a stand. Sometimes it isn't. This classifies me as a pluralist! But it

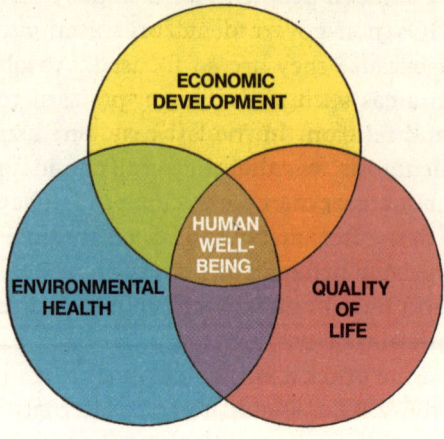

Chart 47 *(Huntley, Siegfried and Sunter)*

means that the kind of tranquil internationalism, which kindly hordes of liberals, new-agers and one-worlders believe in, is never going to eventuate. There will always be people on the outer fringe of competing belief systems who will cause tension in society.

The fourth force shaping the business environment we call the "Wizard of Oz revealed". For those who are too young to have seen the movie with Judy Garland playing a young girl, Dorothy, let me explain. Dorothy travels down the yellow brick road in her scarlet shoes to Emerald City with Tin Man, Scarecrow and Lion. They were off to see the great and powerful Wizard of Oz in order that Tin Man could acquire a heart, Scarecrow a brain and Lion courage. When they were ushered into the room and Dorothy presented the broomstick of the wicked Witch of the West to the Wizard, he boomed out some thunderous pronouncements from behind a curtain which made them quake and cower. These pronouncements were accompanied by smoke and fire and terrible images of his face. Then Dorothy's dog, Toto, trotted forward and pulled back the curtain behind which the great and powerful Oz was concealed. This revealed a small, avuncular old man talking into a big megaphone. Dorothy was obviously very irritated and accused the Wizard of being a very bad man; to which the Wizard replied: "Oh no, my dear, I'm a very good man. I'm just a very bad Wizard!" Alas, his mystery was forever destroyed.

This kind of revelation is occurring every day in the world, given the power and universality of the modern media. It is the source of much of our moral and ethical confusion. Politicians, the judiciary, huge corporations and even Prince Charles have gone through the experience of the Wizard of Oz. The magic disappears. It is no coincidence that the ex-leaders of several countries and many captains of industry have been arrested and put on trial for corruption.

3.4 COMPANY TO BELIEVE IN

This brings me to the last point of *Chart 45*. You now have to be a company that people believe in. That applies to both customers and employees. This sounds ironic in an age of an ethics gap, but it remains true. *C'est la vie!* One need only look at the recent uproar in the United States about American companies that subcontract part of their production – be it garments, carpets, sports shoes or soccer balls – to companies that use child labour elsewhere in the world. Celebrities who sponsor these products have been asked live on camera how they feel about twelve-year-old kids working sixteen-hour days in crowded and unsafe conditions where they are subjected to constant verbal and physical abuse and earn a pittance. They have no answer. It is no longer possible to conceal a dirty trick here or a backwater there from the world's press.

On a different note, a British brewer recently introduced a new tangerine-flavoured alcoholic drink called "Thickhead". The public outcry against a label designed to appeal to teenagers forced the company to agree to modify it. What is different is that *The Daily Telegraph* in its editorial gave the name and address of the CEO and urged parents to write to him expressing their disgust.

Governments and countries are not immune either. Sweden, which has always prided itself on taking a thoroughly moral line in international affairs, must have been highly embarrassed by recent statements in newsjournals drawing attention to the fact that it is the only country in Europe – bar Albania – where possession of child pornography is legal! How do you answer that one? You do something about it. But the media reserves its sharpest scalpel for business. With the disclosure of CEOs' salaries in the United States, much print has been devoted to the increases in salaries and other emoluments that CEOs have received in the companies where there have been substantial lay-offs. One article went so far as to call them "The Hit Men". Though turn-of-the-century banker J. P. Morgan argued that a CEO should never make more than twenty times the average salary of a company's employees, the ratio is approaching 185 to 1 for the Fortune 500 companies. The growing inequality in compensation between top and bottom has become a big issue.

3.5 NEW REALITY

Chart 48 summarises the difference between a modern and a postmodern society and is appropriately titled "Reality isn't what it used to be". Whereas in a modern society the mass manufacture of hard objects was the dominant money earner, the provision of information and services is emerging as the principal source of wealth creation. The shift to information and services from manufacturing is as much of a disruption to society as the movement from agriculture to manufacturing was at the beginning of this century. Half of all Americans were employed in agriculture in 1900. The figure is 3 per cent today. Half of all Americans were employed on mass production lines in the 1950s. Only 15 per cent are today. Hence, information and services have become the primary source of job creation. The difference is that in these areas the majority of people are self-employed entrepreneurs or work in small businesses. This has intensified the disaggregation of society.

People and capital used to be restricted in their movements. Now, despite immigration and exchange controls, both are relatively free to move anywhere anytime. Bad government of any nation leads to losses of skilled personnel and capital as never before.

REALITY ISN'T WHAT IT USED TO BE

Industrial (modern) society	Postindustrial (postmodern) society
Economic	
Wealth creation: manufacturing	Wealth creation: information / service
Restricted capital & people movements	Unrestricted capital & people movements
Social / consumers	
Authority vested in stable institutions	Institutional authority questioned Transference to media power
Hierarchical, deferential social order	Egalitarian social order tribes
Handed-down, inherited values	Discovered individual values
Status reflected by things / externals	Status reflected by experiences / internals
National lifestyles	Mixtures of global lifestyles / bazaars
Controlled / closed media	Open / free-access media
Passive consumers	Active / educated / moral consumers
Marketing / business	
Business activities backstage (covert)	Business activities frontstage and transparent (overt)
Mass Media	Fragmented specialist media
National markets	Global markets
Mass marketing	Mass customisation / relationship marketing

Chart 48 *(Lannon)*

Authority used to be vested in stable institutions, but it is being increasingly transferred to "media power". CNN's star correspondent, Christiane Amanpour, recently graced the cover of *Newsweek* as the first lady of global TV. Reporters are now greater celebrities than most of the people they interview.

Hierarchal deferential social order has been replaced by "egalitarian social order tribes". An example of the latter would be Liverpool supporters.

Handed-down inherited values are now discovered on the Internet. In the old days if your child asked you a question at supper in the kitchen you would give him an answer and he would accept it as handed-down family wisdom. Now, he will leave the table and e-mail his pal in Thailand and come back half an hour later and say: "You're wrong! My friend in Thailand says this." Singapore faces the problem that they don't like a lot of what is on the Internet. But they want to keep up with the modern world. So what do they do? Singapore has become the first country to attempt to use technology to stop its citizens viewing undesirable material in cyberspace. However, this attempt may fail because the Internet – uncontrolled and uncontrollable – crosses borders, linking people one to one.

Status used to be reflected by external things, but is more and more being reflected by experiences. Did you know that ten million Japanese go ballroom dancing over the weekend? They prefer that to buying fancy cars. In fact, there is a backlash against mass-produced hard objects because they are the antithesis of individuality and self-expression. People want soft experiences which are emotional and full of personal meaning.

National lifestyles are being supplanted by mixtures of global lifestyles and bazaars of competing ideologies.

What were once controlled, closed media are now open, free-access media. At the same time, passive consumers have become active, educated, moral consumers. Given the sheer unfettered pervasiveness of the media, the watchful eyes of organised and highly motivated consumer groups and the more inquiring mind-set and investigative skills of consumers, manufacturers can't work to double standards any more. They will be caught out.

So, business activities – backstage and covert – must now be frontstage and transparent. No more skilful manipulation of the strings behind the curtain. That was pre-CNN.

I recently watched a programme on British television aired at prime time on a Saturday evening. It started with a reporter buying free-range eggs from a well-known supermarket chain. He then went to one of the farms from which the eggs were sourced and filmed the shed in which the chickens were crammed. It looked like any old battery farm. When the farmer was asked how he could possibly call his operation free-range, he pointed to a door at the far end of the shed and said that the chickens could theoretically climb over one another to get into a small yard outside.

The scene then switched to the pavement outside the supermarket. As soon as a housewife appeared who had purchased the free-range eggs, the reporter collared her and asked her how she visualised the farm that the eggs had come from. She said that she pictured chickens being able to meander freely around a large yard in a natural setting, pecking seeds as they went. That was why she paid the extra 20p for the eggs. The reporter then depressed the "play" button on a VCR installed outside the shop and the housewife was filmed watching the video of the actual circumstances in which the eggs were laid. As expected, she reacted in a horrified way and said that she would never buy those eggs again. A senior member of the Egg Board was then interviewed about the apparent contradiction between the terminology used on the package and the actual situation. He merely replied that it depended on how you define the words "free" and "range"!

In the corporate world, therefore, many new "Davids" are challenging the established "Goliaths" on the grounds that consumers want to look through the products and see an attractive company behind them (Richard Branson and Anita Roddick would qualify as "Davids"). They want to purchase the right social values as well. The latter not only cover the working conditions of employees, but also the company's attitude towards the environment and the humane treatment of animals. Feel-good labels and brands are not enough. Customers want explicit codes of conduct from the companies they're buying from. Thus, companies may soon have to do ethical audits as well as financial ones. In the public relations field, they already talk of "reputation management".

Mass media have become fragmented specialist media. For example, 90 per cent of Americans used to watch prime-time news on the three major television networks. Now only 40 per cent do and only 20 per cent of the young. The remainder are watching MTV or sports channels or seeking enjoyment in other forms of entertainment. Multi-choice satellite television, specialist newspapers, journals and radio stations are blossoming. This makes any advertising campaign much more difficult to conceive. It could just be that the "prime-time" slot that you choose for your advertisement is being watched by very few people.

National markets are being superseded by global markets. In Israel young entrepreneurs first think of the American market as a place to launch their products. If they make a bit of money in Tel Aviv too, that is the cherry on top. They have incredible "chutzpah" – a can-do spirit epitomised by an Israeli T-shirt that reads: "Don't worry America, Israel is behind you". In South Africa, we have exactly the opposite mentality amongst most of our entrepreneurs. They will market a product in South Africa, and if it is a success they will seek to supplement their income overseas. We have not yet acquired a global consciousness.

Finally, mass marketing is giving way to mass customisation and relationship marketing. Not so long ago companies followed Henry Ford's dictum: "You can have any colour you want, provided it's black." He could sell cars that way because the public, faced with a limited number of options, were relatively undiscriminating. But now we have a new mass elite – one billion middle-class citizens in the world – demanding that their every whim be catered for. Moreover, they want to be pampered with the same level of individualised service that the old, tiny elite got. Not for nothing does the Internet call this turn of events "the market of one".

This logically leads to relationship marketing. We have moved beyond "tell me which colour you want and I'll provide it" to "Let you and me sit down and discuss the choice". Essentially, you are now appealing to the subjective personal side of customers. They are more likely to stay loyal to you if you relate to them as individuals, demonstrate gratitude for their custom and do something extra. In the United States, American cars have caught up with Japanese cars in terms of quality. Hence, a recent survey showed that the factor which determines the choice of model for an American consumer is after-sales service. Moreover, relationship marketing demands feminine gender characteristics as indicated in *Chart 49*. These characteristics have meant that women in both America and Britain are now more successful than men in opening up and running small businesses. Female entrepreneurs shun the male-dominated world of big business. As such, in many countries they now represent the most powerful and inspirational force behind economic growth (particularly because

GENDER VALUES & DOMINANT BUSINESS CULTURE

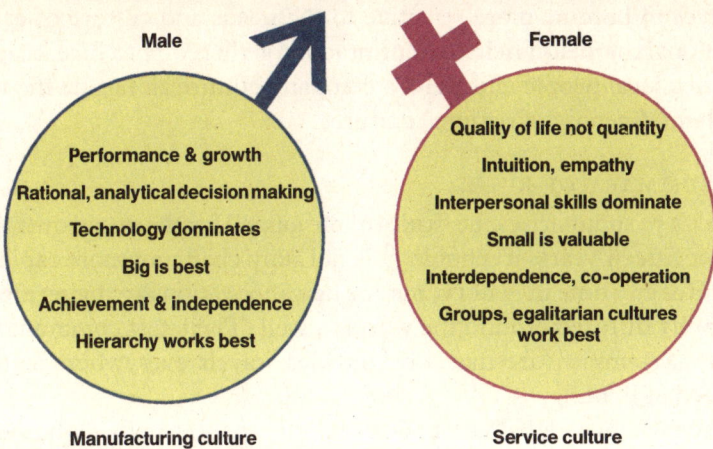

Chart 49 (Lannon)

service businesses, which they're comparatively better at running than men, now constitute about 70 per cent of GDP).

Bangladesh is an unusual example, where 97 per cent of the borrowers from the Grameen Bank, a bank that specialises in loans to microbusinesses, are women. According to *The Economist*, since 1987 in America the number of businesses owned by women has increased by 78 per cent to eight million – representing one-third of all firms – and their number is growing at double the rate of firms owned by men. Women-owned firms also have more staying power than the average; three-quarters of those that existed in 1991 were still alive three years later, compared with two-thirds of all American companies. The number of people employed in women-owned companies that have a hundred or more workers is rising more than twice as fast as the average for all such American firms. Right now, women-owned businesses of all sizes employ 18,5 million people, or one out of four American workers. Certainly, at this rate, women will be the biggest beneficiaries of a postmodernist society. But like all things, there is a downside. Families will be the biggest casualties: househusbands are not as good at bringing up children.

Another consequence of mass customisation and relationship marketing is that world-class companies are restructuring themselves to become more sensitive to the needs and culture of each national market. Their current practice is therefore to hire imaginative local people and build a company culture alongside the resultant diversity of national cultures.

4 SUMMARY OF RULES

Chart 50 summarises the "rules of the game" for the world over the next fifteen years. Technology is not only changing more rapidly than at any time in history, but the new innovations are being more rapidly diffused around the world as well. The latest communication systems ensure that a bright idea travels everywhere at the speed of light.

We live in a global village and markets are now truly globalised.

RULES OF THE GAME

* **TECHNOLOGY**	rapid change, rapid diffusion
* **GLOBALISATION**	through market systems
* **DEMOGRAPHY**	long-term ageing; lower real interest rates
* **VALUES**	complex and capricious power of NGOs
* **INTERDEPENDENCE**	for good & ill
* **ENVIRONMENTAL CONCERNS**	risks & opportunities for business
* **WINNERS & LOSERS**	increasing penalties for failure
* **COLOMBIANISATION**	insidious, global

Chart 50 (AAC Research and Economic Services Dept., London)

This applies to goods, services, currencies, shares, bonds, etc. It has even prompted James Carville, who directed Bill Clinton's campaign in 1992, to make the famous remark: "I used to think that if there was reincarnation, I wanted to come back as the president, or the pope. But now I want to be the bond market: you can intimidate everybody." Certainly, any government that makes a bad policy decision is quickly punished by the market.

The key implications of the latest demographic trends are the long-term ageing of the world's population and lower real interest rates because of additional high-saving middle-aged people. This rule clearly does not apply to the countries worst affected by AIDS.

Values are complex and capricious. The power of single-issue NGOs must not be underestimated. The National Rifle Association in America wields awesome power. Greenpeace, with its annual budget of around $143 million from almost three million dues-paying members, is now one of the most influential bodies in the world. It took on the world's most profitable company – Royal Dutch Shell – over where the Brent Spar oil rig should be disposed of, and won the first round. Shell had planned to sink the rig at sea, but cancelled its plan after Greenpeace mobilised public opinion against it. Greenpeace wanted it dismantled on land. Currently, the oil rig is sitting in a Norwegian fjord whilst further studies are undertaken. The incident showed the vulnerability of multinational companies and governments to narrowly based belief groups who can turn an issue into a *cause célèbre*.

The world is becoming more interdependent for good and ill. Worldwide foreign direct investment increased by 46 per cent between 1994 and 1995 to set a new record level of $325 billion. The rich industrialised countries attracted $216 billion. Developing countries registered investment inflows of $97 billion, an all-time high. China, Indonesia, Malaysia and Thailand won the lion's share of such investment. The transition economies of Central and Eastern Europe recorded inflows of $12 billion – twice as much as the previous year and the highest figure ever. Cross-border mergers, acquisitions and alliances are proceeding apace. Meanwhile, international trade continues to outstrip the growth in the world economy.

As can be seen from the earlier section on global warming, environmental concerns are going to feature much more on the agenda of business. This offers both risks and opportunities. Certainly because of media power, businesses will not get away with polluting any part of the globe for long – even if it is a remote area.

Any country or company that does not understand and follow these rules of the game will be subject to increasing penalties for failure. In this hyper-competitive world, companies will not just see their profits reduced, they will go bankrupt. Should they tarnish their reputations in any other way, the incident will never be forgotten. If nations do not adopt the formula for a "winning nation", they will not just lose; they will vanish from the radar screen. Of the 200 countries in the world, 70 countries have lower average incomes than they did in 1980 and 43 are poorer than they were in 1970. So the gap between winners and losers has already widened. That trend could now accelerate.

Finally, it was Edouard Parker, our remarkable French consultant, who first drew our team's attention to "Colombianisation" – a term he coined in the late 1980s to describe the increasing criminality of the world. Colombia is well known for its drug cartels, the power they wield and the anarchy they cause. To begin with, we were sceptical about Edouard's theory. But each year that passes has brought further confirmation that Colombianisation is insidious and global. Drugs are now the second biggest business in the world after tourism and before defence. The top 25 Mafia families in the US earned $64 billion last year out of drugs – before and after tax. This final rule means that at some time during our scenario period of fifteen years international criminal syndicates could end up wielding as much power as legal governments. At the same time, given its location, South Africa could become an entrepôt for the drug traffic between East and West. Nigerian gangs have already set up shop here.

A noted military journalist in England, John Keegan, would beg to differ with this analysis. Yes, he would say, lawlessness is rife outside the Western world and it does threaten us. Yes, it is possible to imagine a society falling prey to criminals and fanatics.

But what would be the reaction of the oppressed majority? People, as Hobbes pointed out in the eighteenth century, cannot tolerate chronic insecurity. They need peace as much as they need food. If denied it, they will not only give their loyalty to anyone who can assure it, they will also sanction any measure that this "Leviathan" – as Hobbes called the bringer of security – deems necessary to restore order. All, therefore, that Colombianisation will do is to turn democratic states temporarily into totalitarian ones until the criminals are rooted out.

The "Key Uncertainties"

Having reduced the cone of uncertainty that opens up over the next fifteen years by establishing the "rules of the game", we now look at the "key uncertainties". *Chart 51* lists them.

The most important question to be asked is: Who is going to maintain world order from now on? We used to have empires that brought stability to large areas of the world. For example, we had a Greek, a Roman, an Ottoman and a British empire. Then we had two superpowers. But the Soviet Union dissolved itself in the late 1980s and America went on an expedition into Somalia (where the troops arrived after the CNN cameras). Neither that war nor the ones in Vietnam and the Gulf provide happy reminiscences for the American public. The media have made the horror of war far more visible to American mothers. The upshot is that America's direct interests have to be severely threatened for the despatch of troops overseas to be justified in the public eye. As a substitute, America

KEY UNCERTAINTIES

* **GEOPOLITICAL**	**Maintaining world order. Who?** **Nightmare visions**
* **GEONOMIC**	**TRIAD tensions** **OECD versus Non-OECD**
* **SOCIETAL**	**OECD** – **the underclass &** **the insecure employed** – **loss of social cohesion** – **Japan regression?** **RUSSIA & CHINA** – **capacity for modernisation?**

Chart 51 (AAC Research and Economic Services Dept., London)

occasionally uses high-tech remote forms of delivery like long-range cruise missiles as a risk-free means of attacking an adversary. However, missiles without men have limited impact. America is being forced to become more circumspect about taking the lead in international affairs just when the ratio of stable to unstable states in the world has hit an all-time low of 24 out of 200.

The United Nations, which many people regard as the best substitute for an individual superpower, doesn't have the funds to exercise an effective role as global cop. Its resources are already thinly spread in the hot spots of the world. Moreover, when the bullets really fly, UN troops have to look on in a helpless fashion. The era that we are moving into has variously been described as the New World Disorder or the New Middle Ages. This sounds ironic in an age where the rich nations have nuclear weapons. But the kind of global disorder that exists – which is variously caused by left-wing terrorist groups, fanatic religious movements and right-wing militia – requires a totally different form of control. The emphasis has to be on global intelligence networks and rapid reaction anti-terrorist squads, which can fly anywhere at a moment's notice. Nevertheless, a vacuum of authority poses nightmare visions of some tinpot dictator getting hold of a nuclear device and holding the rest of the world to ransom.

On the economic front, the "key uncertainties" revolve around whether the world will move smoothly towards a frictionless international trading system or whether nationalisation and protectionism will get in the way. We may well see further tensions among the three members of the Triad, namely Western Europe, North America and Japan. In 1995, Japan and America came very close to a full-scale trade war over the importation of car parts into Japan. In 1996, there has been a huge row between Britain and the other nations of the European Union over how many cattle should be slaughtered to minimise the threat of mad cow disease being passed on to human beings.

But it is not just the relationship between the rich nations that can throw a spanner in the works of free trade. There may also be shocks to the system from developed and developing countries falling out. A case in point is the recent dispute between China and the United States over pirated CDs and tapes being produced in China. Moreover, a threat always exists that rich countries may clamp down on the exports of poor countries if they feel that the goods are being dumped in their domestic market at abnormally low prices and are thereby causing unemployment. All in all, despite the establishment of the World Trade Organisation, it could be a rocky road ahead for international trade.

As far as societal trends are concerned, we don't just have the underclass of the unemployed. They have been joined by the insecure employed. This mainly applies to white-collar workers whose jobs used to be protected from international competition. Now virtually all jobs are contestable. For example, British insurance companies are subcontracting their back-room operations to Indian companies in India. This means that Indian clerks are now putting British clerks out of work. A local authority in England put out a tender not so long ago for the keeping of its archives. This was won by a company in Taiwan. The transactions are e-mailed on a daily basis to Taiwan for collation and classification and e-mailed back the following day. Will Hutton, in his book *The State We're In*, reckoned that 30 per cent of the British workforce could be classified as the insecure employed while another 30 per cent were thoroughly disadvantaged with no job at all or part-time work. Only 40 per cent qualified as the privileged class with education, jobs, housing and pensions. Because of this trend, middle management in both America and Britain are working longer hours and taking shorter holidays to the extent that they are now called the "hard-working class".

The loss of social cohesion brings uncertainties because of the authority and ethics gaps. How are the increasing number of middle-aged and elderly people going to cope with the amoral and anarchic youth? In order to overcome their anxieties and fears, will they vote in a Hitlerian-type dictator who promises to restore law and order through repressive measures; or will the kids be allowed to continue to roam the streets in an unrestrained way? Will one see a greater number of people seeking a more secure existence by joining one of the more extreme religious movements?

Japan has suffered a tremendous psychological blow since the mid-1980s. At that time, the country was considered the out-and-out winner of the global economy and destined to soar into the 1990s. America, because of its short-termism, was expected to falter. Our scenario team fell into the trap of going along with this mainstream thinking. However, quite the reverse has happened. American industry has gone through an incredible renaissance and the United States once again has an unchallenged predominance in the world economy. Take capital productivity: a unit of capital in America delivers about half as much output again as an equivalent amount of spending in either Germany or Japan. Meanwhile, Japan has regressed. The bubble of astronomical property and share values was pricked in 1990. On some measurements, the property market fell by as much as 80 per cent when it hit its low and the share market fell by half. The fall was equivalent to three times Japan's GDP in the case of property and to Japan's GDP in the case of shares. Neither crash is surprising in retrospect. The Imperial Palace in Tokyo was at one stage worth more in real estate value than the entire state of California, and pedestrian shares had price/earning ratios in excess of 100.

So, the scale of asset deflation in Japan has been staggering. Serious restructuring of industry has yet to occur. For example, car industry employment has fallen by only 8 per cent while output has fallen from 13,5 million units to 9,5 million units. It is now estimated that there are three million workers (5 per cent of total employment) surplus to requirements in manufacturing alone. Japan must restructure and the jobs lost in industry need to be replaced by new service sector businesses.

High profile cases of corruption amongst top-ranking politicians and officials have been exposed. The country is in as bad a shape as Italy, with public debt at 100 per cent of GDP (against a recommended level in the European Union of 60 per cent). These factors, together with the Kobe earthquake, the subway nerve-gas attack, the HIV contamination of blood products and the recent bout of food poisoning in schools, have led Japan back into a state of extreme angst. While observers believe that Japan has turned the corner and is now heading back to the kind of economic growth rates it achieved in the 1980s, it is too soon to tell.

At the moment, two of the largest countries in the world – Russia and China – are in a state of transition from pre-modern to modern societies. There is a critical difference between them. Russia has made the transition to democracy but has a malperforming economy. China has had a brilliant economic run but has not yet converted to multiparty democracy. Either case has its own dangers. Democracy without economic success can lead to a disillusioned electorate voting in bad leaders, and economic success without democracy can lead to a clash between incumbent rulers wishing to preserve their power and an electorate wanting more freedom of political choice.

Currently, politics are highly personalised in both countries. This leads to a greater ad-hoccery and unpredictability in policy formulation, together with ministerial and other senior political appointments, than in a country with established institutions that check and balance each other. Capitalism in both countries is at an early stage of development. Property rights are insecure and the rule of law is inconsistently applied. In particular, uncertainty surrounds company law, including tax and foreign investment codes, which makes it difficult to do business. Corruption is rife, with the spoils created by the transition being divided among the elite. Criminal Mafias which number among their members many ex-party officials have eagerly filled any vacuum left by the state in retreating from its formerly dominant role in the economy.

Two broad long-term scenarios apply to both Russia and China: "liberalisation" or "strongman". Either the two countries progress bumpily from the robber-baron-type capitalism that they have now to a modern free-enterprise society in the next century (like the US did at the end of the last one). At the same time, China switches from one-party rule to multiparty politics. This is the liberalisation or soft-landing scenario. Or they revert to repressive, authoritarian states with a strong man in charge. Such a strong man may well reject Western models of economic development and pursue his own particular ideology. This scenario implies two possible outcomes: the ruler is strong enough to hold the place together through terror, or ultimately he is incapable of doing so, in which case the country fragments. Of course, one country may go down one path, while the other chooses the alternative. Whatever the future holds, the world will remain a highly uncertain place while the destinies of two of its biggest players remain unresolved. Any domestic shocks in either country will have global repercussions.

The Global Scenarios

The next step is to flex the "key uncertainties" within the boundary of possibilities drawn by the "rules of the game". *Chart 52* depicts the resultant global scenarios over the next fifteen years. Basically, there are two mainstream scenarios – "convergence" and "divergence". This may sound vague but it is much better to be vaguely right than precisely wrong! At the top, the forces pushing the world towards a more prosperous future are the usual mantra given by economists of globalisation, deregulation and liberalisation. This, together with technology, interaction and interdependence, compels the world to coalesce around a universal economic model. The only question is "whose"? Will it be the highly individualistic American model, or will it be the team model of the Far East? One company called the forces driving the world towards a universal model "Hurricane Tina", where Tina means "there is no alternative" – a favourite phrase of Maggie Thatcher. Hurricane Tina

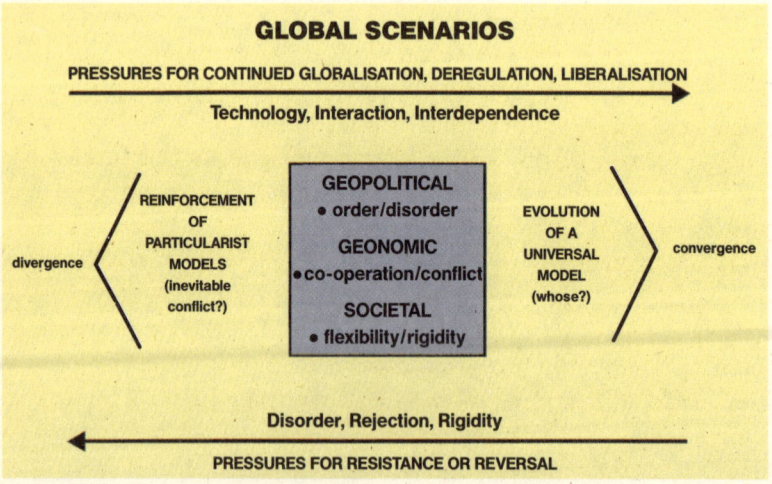

Chart 52 *(AAC Research and Economic Services Dept. London)*

will blow down the barricades of all countries, including those which have tried to seal themselves off from the world like Myanmar (formerly Burma), North Korea, Albania and Cuba.

Our scenario team feels that it is premature to pin all one's hopes on such a future, i.e. the fifth Kondratieff wave. As *Chart 52* shows, there are major pressures for resistance or reversal which could lead to a much more sinister, fragmented world. In this scenario, economic harmonisation would be more than offset by political diversification where people splinter into ever smaller nation states. Moreover, the persistent problems of social inequity between countries as well as between the classes within each country become a fertile ground for discontent and violence. Rich nations battle to keep illegal immigrants at bay and the relatively disadvantaged in their own societies at peace. Criminals foment the violence to their own advantage.

Hence, disorder may easily flow from the authority vacuum in the world. It is perfectly possible, given the personalism of politics in either Russia or China, for a new leader who rejects Western models of economic development to emerge and come up with his own particular model. After all, the practical free-enterprise model can easily be made to look defective. Success relies on individual effort and therefore no automatic paradise – no Utopia – beckons. Marxism made the mistake of offering paradise on Earth, but Islam doesn't and therefore has much greater staying power. Islam might play a role in upsetting the apple cart of the Middle East. A country like Saudi Arabia could be vulnerable and go the way of Iran. Finally, many societies have a fundamental rigidity which gets in the way of technologies creating a better world.

If one had been a scenario thinker at the beginning of this century, it would have been so easy to lay out just the positive scenario. New technologies such as electricity, the internal combustion engine and steamships were creating the third Kondratieff wave. Foreign investment and world trade were booming. One would have been right for fourteen years. The Edwardian age was golden. Then the First World War started and one would have been wrong. So here we are at the next *fin de siècle*, and it would be unwise to make the same mistake. The world as always is finely balanced between the forces of good and evil, of sanity and insanity. If another Great War breaks out, it could begin in the Middle East or perhaps the Far East, where China is becoming more imperialistic and might provoke a war with its neighbours. The latter is more likely to develop into a genuine Third World War because of the weapons build-up taking place in that area of the globe. Nowhere else are countries so eagerly stocking up with the latest and most lethal weapons of war. So don't just presume that the Far East is a wonderful, well-oiled, economic machine that will purr along into the next century. There could be shocks. Never before in history have the archrivals, China and Japan, been successful and powerful at the same time. Indonesia is restless too.

The only principle that may stop such a scenario is ironically called "MAD" – mutually assured destruction with nuclear weapons. It could be construed as a "rule of the game" which permits no further global confrontations. However, the risk remains of misinformation or misjudgment causing one side rashly to push the button first.

In a divergent world, America will clearly distinguish between its friends and enemies. South Africa will have to be very careful in choosing the countries that it allies itself with. Equally, multinational companies may become important stabilisers as the only institutions left with empires that cross borders. Microsoft replaces Rome.

The South African Scenarios

Against the background of the latest "rules of the game", "key uncertainties" and scenarios for the world, what are the options for South Africa? *Chart 53* is one that I used in my original presentation in 1986. It was put together by Michael O'Dowd and Bobby Godsell and has certainly proved relevant over the last ten years. However, what makes the chart a stroke of genius is that I can include it now and it is relevant for the next ten years as well.

On the vertical axis one has high, low and negative economic growth. Across the top are various kinds of society. On the left-hand side you have a society where the group dominates over the individual; in other words a racially polarised society. In the middle you have a society in transition and on the right-hand side a society where the individual matters more than the group. The

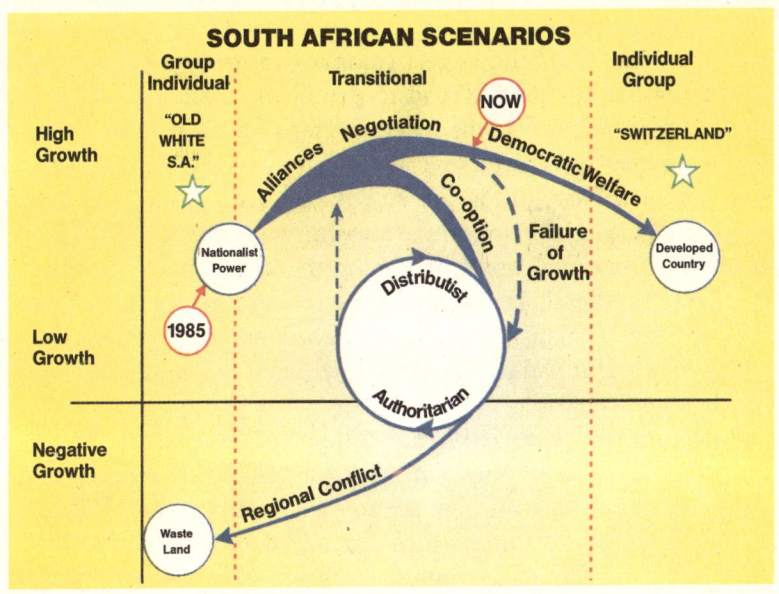

Chart 53 *(O'Dowd and Godsell)*

last is a nonracial society, but an element of group consciousness persists. For example, America has a very individualistic society, but people still have group loyalties as Italian-Americans, African-Americans, Chinese-Americans, etc.

In 1985, when the chart was originally formulated, the National Party sat on the edge of transition. Many people at the time had the desire to return to the "Old White South Africa", but we regarded it as an unfulfillable dream. Hence, we depicted it as a green star. Instead we maintained that the National Party had to go into transition and it was the nature of the alliances which it formed that would determine the course of South Africa in the near term. The National Party could either negotiate with the real leaders or co-opt a bunch of tame representatives into government. The former option would allow economic growth to rise as South Africa returned to the global fold. We called it the "High Road". The latter option would spark off a revolt by the masses, in which event South Africa would head downhill and take the "Low Road".

I remember that many audiences in 1986 regarded the negotiation route as a pipe dream. In fact, some people remarked that it was irresponsible of the largest company in South Africa to send somebody like me on the road to peddle such fantasy. After all, no group in the world had ever negotiated themselves out of power on their own turf! Nevertheless, the fantasy became reality. The National Party did negotiate with the ANC and, after an appropriate period of being in partnership with the ANC in a government of national unity, it is now the chief opposition party. Incidentally, the chart illustrates the strength of scenario thinking, because for many people the "High Road" of negotiation was unthinkable. If it had not happened, we would of course have said it was just a scenario!

So where are we now? We are still on the "High Road" but at the second fork in the diagram. Are we going to continue across the top of the chart with high economic growth? Then we can become a developed country which can afford to dispense welfare to the really disadvantaged communities. You will see a star adjacent to where we splash down as a developed country after emerging from the transition. It is entitled "Switzerland". Again, this is a dream because South Africa will never be exactly like Switzerland. On the other hand, Switzerland has been home to a wide diversity of people who have not fought a war with one another in 700 years. It is therefore a good model to aim for.

Alternatively, are we going to have a failure of economic growth because of a world recession, a drop in the gold price or because we shoot ourselves in the foot with the wrong economic policies? Failure of economic growth will mean that we suffer the same dismal fate as we would have experienced if we had taken the wrong political path. You can see the arrow bending towards the left since failure will inevitably lead to the old rifts in society reappearing. People will become polarised as they blame each other for the failure. Extremists trump moderates in the "Low Road" scenario and life becomes a zero-sum game of "if I win, you lose" and "winner takes all".

On account of rising unemployment leading to an escalation in unrest and violent crime, the South African government has no option but to crack down. We enter an authoritarian phase. Then a popular hero or heroine arises to challenge the authoritarian state and promises redistribution of wealth to the masses. These promises fail to materialise and we return to another authoritarian period. And so one goes around the vicious circle in the middle of the chart like clothes in a washing machine. We call this the "Argentinian Tango" because for a long time after the Second World War Argentina alternated between the generals and the Perons (Juan and Eva and then Isabel). Luckily, the country has managed to get out of this vicious circle and ascend up the dotted path on the left of the circle. It is now considered one of the more successful nations in South America, having ditched the dirigisme and socialism of the 1970s for the free-market policies of today.

However, the more likely result of tumbling around in the circle is that the institutions associated with a civil society will be destroyed. A civil society was a concept that emerged in the eighteenth century with the parallel growth of market capitalism and bourgeois society. It was a name given by Scottish philosophers to distinguish the new order from savage and barbaric societies. A civil society was civilised and ordered by the rule of law. It was large-scale and held together by impersonal bonds of interest rather than ties of kin and blood. It was characterised by a variety of institutions and voluntary associations intermediate in size between that of the state and the family. While it was not necessarily democratic, rule of law and a regular government were crucial. In a civil society the middle class prospered.

Be that as it may, let's return to the centre of the diagram. The tango between authoritarianism and populism grinds the middle class into the dust and what remains is an aristocratic elite and an angry proletariat. After several turns around the circle, it is quite possible that whatever government is in power lacks the necessary force to hold the state together. One then spins off down the path to the left, into a regional conflict between rival warlords. The result is a highly criminalised, racially and ethnically polarised wasteland in the bottom left-hand corner of the chart. The economic growth rate by this time is substantially negative because the place has been torn to shreds. South Africa ceases to exist. It becomes a patchwork of impoverished fiefdoms. Paradise lost.

We are now at the economic, as opposed to the political, crossroads. This is why economic growth is so crucial to our future at this juncture. It is not that difficult to achieve annual growth of at least 6 per cent. The less developed countries exceeded that figure from 1950 to 1995 except for the period 1980 to 1985 (when it was 4 per cent). We have been very lucky to have Nelson Mandela as our President, because he has legendary status and has acted as the glue to hold the country together. But, as a legend, he is irreplaceable. So the glue has to change. The path across the top of the chart assumes that when Nelson Mandela goes, the glue that holds the country together is economic success. In all other "winning nations" in the world, people are not overly worried about who the leader is as they are too busy creating wealth for themselves and their families or doing other things. In our case, success will also blur the old lines of colour, ethnicity and language since individuals will see themselves as part of a winning rainbow team. An excellent illustration of this principle at work was the recent victory of Bafana Bafana in the African Nations Soccer

Cup. The victory itself not only moulded the soccer stars who took part in the matches into a highly co-ordinated and well-knit team, but it was also an important symbol in uniting the nation.

Two other important conclusions flow from this chart. The first is that you can't indulge in a major programme of redistribution and welfare before you have experienced a period of high economic growth. That is why democratic welfare is shown towards the end of the "High Road" trajectory. You have to earn the money before you spend it. The second implication is that trade unions should be as interested in a positive outcome as business because there is no authoritarian regime anywhere in the world that tolerates trade unions. If the country slides down the dotted "failure of growth" line, Cosatu will suffer along with everybody else. Indeed, the history of the twentieth century has shown the dangers for everyone of a nation entering a period of general wretchedness. Both Mussolini and Hitler were elected by the unemployed to improve their lot.

Nonetheless, the trade unions can play a very positive role on the "High Road" path. Indeed, they are an integral part of a free-enterprise society since workers in such a society have the right of freedom of association. If the unions wish to expand their membership, they will have to play a wider role in representing their members' direct interests in society. In other words, they should be using their negotiating clout not only to provide the best conditions of employment for their members, but they should also be negotiating the best deals in terms of mortgages, holiday packages, insurance, etc. In effect, they should become one-stop negotiation shops for their members – who after all are their customers.

So, what is the vision that will continue to carry us across the top of the chart? *Chart 54* demonstrates emphatically that Europe is the wrong model. It shows the total number of jobs in existence in the economy since 1960. As can be seen, Europe has hardly created any new jobs and its unemployment rate has tripled. If unemployment is regarded as the number one problem in this country, we should rather be imitating North America which has doubled its pool of jobs in the same period. This is because

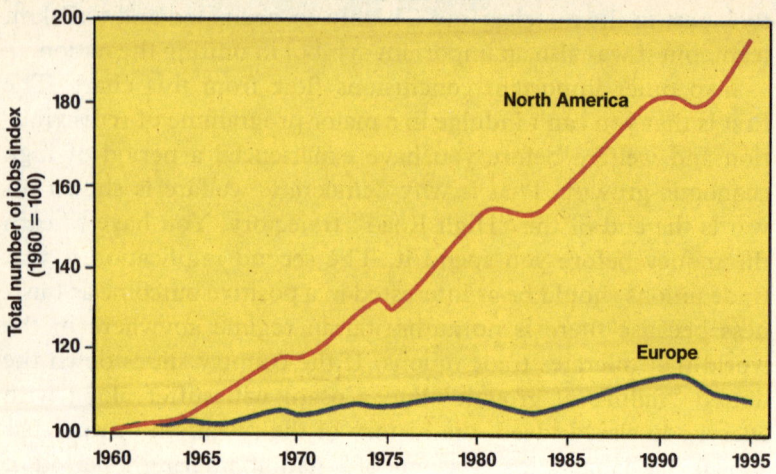

Chart 54 (SA Foundation, "Growth for All")

Americans have a completely different attitude to work. They regard a job like acting in a play. You know that the play is going to come to an end at some time. When the audiences start to dwindle and the box office takings begin to decline, you make plans to move on to another play. The average American has seven careers in his/her lifetime. The key word in America is "employability" rather than "employment". Acting experience and the ability to play a variety of roles – from comedy to tragedy – land you the next part.

Because the commercial market is changing at a faster rate than at any other time in history, flexibility in the job market is essential. This is still not accepted in Europe where lifetime employment with one company and regular hours in predictable patterns are considered the norm and entrenched by labour legislation. How can such inflexibility handle markets that are in perpetual transition? The answer is that it fails miserably.

We therefore need to look at an alternative. *Chart 55* is gleaned from Rosabeth Moss Kanter's book *World Class*. In the knowledge-intensive era that we are now in, it is essential that any nation which wants to be world class develops and maintains three intangible assets:

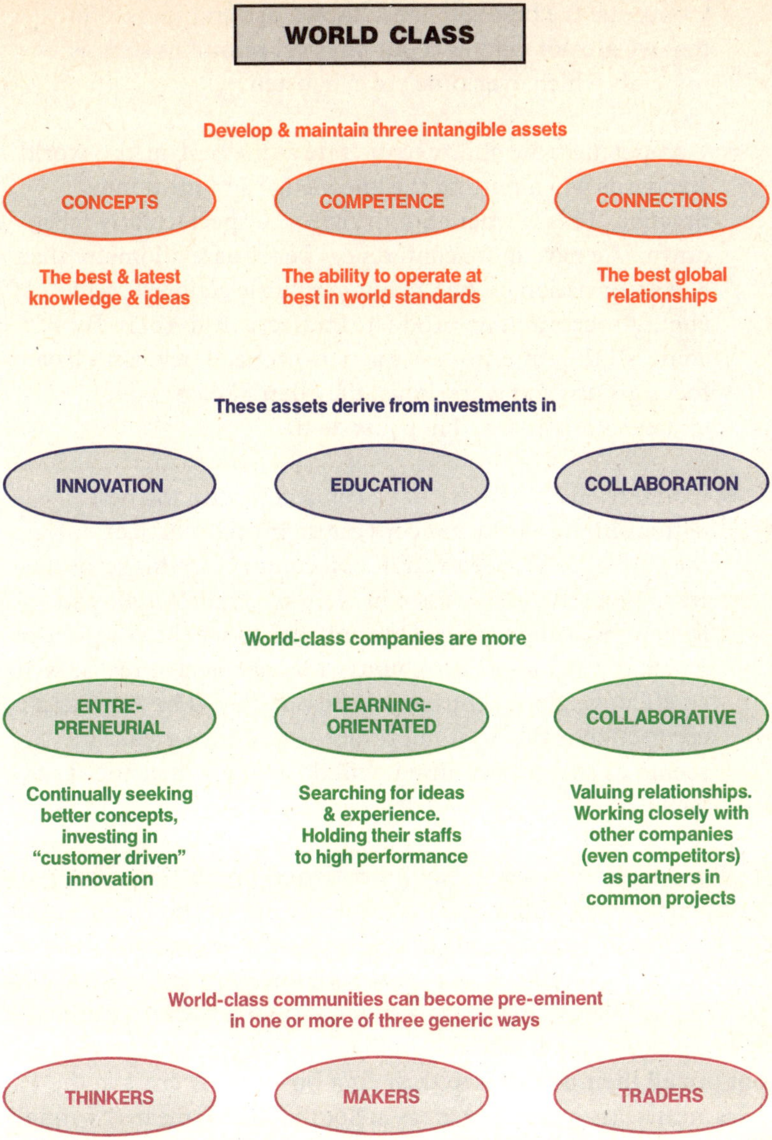

WORLD CLASS

Develop & maintain three intangible assets

- **CONCEPTS** — The best & latest knowledge & ideas
- **COMPETENCE** — The ability to operate at best in world standards
- **CONNECTIONS** — The best global relationships

These assets derive from investments in

- **INNOVATION**
- **EDUCATION**
- **COLLABORATION**

World-class companies are more

- **ENTRE-PRENEURIAL** — Continually seeking better concepts, investing in "customer driven" innovation
- **LEARNING-ORIENTATED** — Searching for ideas & experience. Holding their staffs to high performance
- **COLLABORATIVE** — Valuing relationships. Working closely with other companies (even competitors) as partners in common projects

World-class communities can become pre-eminent in one or more of three generic ways

- **THINKERS**
- **MAKERS**
- **TRADERS**

Chart 55 (Rosabeth Moss Kanter, "World Class")

* **C**oncepts: the best and latest knowledge and ideas. Note that we are not talking about physical resources such as minerals which over time are exhausted.

* **C**ompetence: the ability to operate at the best-in-the-world standards when putting the knowledge and ideas into practice. This is where South Africa so spectacularly falls down. We have more conferences per square kilometre than any other nation on Earth, but very little action. It's all about process and no product. Ineffectualism rules. By contrast, the Americans are action-prone. They don't have focus groups and workshops, they don't boast about strategies and plans. They just do it.

* **C**onnections: You have to be connected with the best nations in the world and copycat their best practices *where* they are of relevance to your own country. In this respect we have an incredible asset in Nelson Mandela, who can forge those connections. One only has to see the enthusiasm which greets him in any country that he visits to realise what an effective globe-trotting role he can play. The American connection is the most important – they have a stake in seeing us succeed because it will do a lot for their society as well.

The three "C's" that I have mentioned are derived from investments in innovation, education and collaboration. We are not yet an innovative society like the Far East. For example, it is the fifth business on average that succeeds in the Far East for a budding entrepreneur. The first four usually go bankrupt, but are used as a steep learning curve. This means that Far Eastern entrepreneurs do not put all their money into their first business. A cross in the Far East means "try again", whereas in South Africa it means "wrong". Business failure here is like drawing the "Chance" card in Monopoly which says: "Go to jail, move directly to jail, do not pass 'Go' and do not collect R200." We have to learn that the gateway to success is often failure. As T. S. Eliot wrote: "Between the idea and the reality... falls the shadow." *Chart 56*, a marvellous diagram produced by Synectics, shows the normal path to innovation. Note particularly the "dark night of the innovator". The great innovators went up many blind alleys before they made their discovery. Perhaps the hard times we are going through are the best prelude to our becoming a "winning nation", because the government will learn from its mistakes. If the price of gold was $1 000 and foreign investment was pouring in, there would be no chance of getting the economic policy right. You need pain to restructure and change for the better.

As far as education is concerned, our scenario team has always maintained that the quality of education is the number one characteristic of a "winning nation". But, at a time when most pupils leaving school have to create jobs for themselves rather than find jobs in the formal sector, education has to have an entrepreneurial element. One is beginning to see some outstanding programmes in this country to teach kids how to be entrepreneurs.

The one that I love to quote is the Wykeham Collegiate School for Girls in Pietermaritzburg. Two young teachers there have

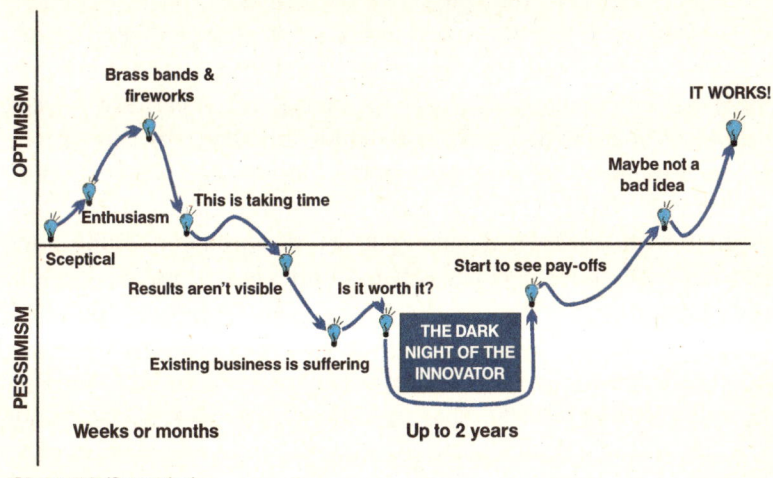

Chart 56 *(Synectics)*

taught the girls to borrow real money from real banks in Pietermaritzburg to open up real businesses, and if those real businesses go bust, real dads bail them out. However, some of the girls are making excellent money out of the goods and services they are selling to the citizens of Pietermaritzburg. They have a market day on weekends at the school. I am told that they even had to ban cellular telephones in class because some of the girls were taking orders rather than listening to the teacher!

In a hyper-competitive world, collaboration is vital because it is impossible to make serious headway on your own. In order for there to be collaboration society has to have trust. It is interesting that in places like China and Taiwan family businesses are the ones that succeed because that is where trust is strongest. However, in Western societies, the evolution of the modern business organisation has been possible because strangers trust one another. South Africa needs collaboration between government and business, because there is only so much the government can do to grow the economy while business can do very little about law and order.

Any "winning nation" has to have its bevy of world-class companies. These are more entrepreneurial than ordinary ones in that they are continually seeking better concepts and investing in "customer-driven" innovation. They are more learning-orientated in that they continually search for ideas and experience which may give them the edge. They hold their staff to high performance, particularly asking them what they've learnt in the last year that is new. So many companies fall down in this crucial area. Of the top 100 companies in the United States in 1956, only one-third are still in the top 100 today. While one cannot be sure of the reasons for their decline, you can be sure of one thing: they didn't predict their decline. It was an unexpected bombshell that did them in.

Success can be blinding. My favourite example is that of Western Union which in 1876 was approached by a young man who said that he had a device that would make the Morse code obsolete. He offered them the patent for the paltry sum of $100 000. Western Union turned him down on the grounds that they were developing a more sophisticated Morse code system. Two years later they went to the young man and offered him $25 million for his device. This time he said, "Thanks, but no thanks, I've started my own company and it's doing rather well." The young man was Alexander Graham Bell, his device was the telephone and Western Union was history. Can you imagine that? The largest company in America in the nineteenth century turned down the telephone, the instrument which is absolutely central to our society today! You have always got to be in a learning frame of mind. The message is simple: keep your radar switched on at all times and never stop conducting 360-degree sweeps of your environment. That way, the twists and turns of life that frustrate you today can be the opportunities of tomorrow.

World-class companies collaborate with one another where necessary even if they are competitors. Many projects today are simply too costly for individual companies to undertake. Rather than merge or take over each other, most world-class companies choose to be partners in common projects. Finally, world-class communities can become pre-eminent in one or more of three generic ways. They can be thinkers, like Boston and Harvard; they can be makers like Detroit and cars; or they can be traders like Singapore and Hong Kong. Johannesburg, for example, could specialise in the thinking and trading category. Some of South Africa's coastal cities will probably remain "makers for export" because businesses can save on internal transportation costs.

It may sound unthinkable for South Africa to become world class given the current shape of its economy, but one must recall how unthinkable the political transition was in the mid-1980s to see that the world-class goal is an eminently sensible one to set ourselves today. When I am asked what the first step towards the achievement of this goal is, I always respond that it must be to create a passion for business in South Africa. We have a passion for politics and for sport, but we have no business heroes or heroines. Among bright young people the usual prime choices of occupation are politician, lawyer and academic. Way down the list is being an entrepreneur – roughly equivalent to being a crook.

There is still an impression in this country that if you are an entrepreneur running a small business, you are only doing this because you have to. The small and microbusiness sectors are considered a refugee camp for those unlucky enough not to find jobs in the formal sector. However, nothing could be further from the truth. Many people who run their own businesses do not want to work in the formal sector, to be a small fish in a large pond or to have a boss telling them what to do. They consider running a small business as an exciting adventure. They obtain more dignity and self-esteem out of being their own boss.

If one looks at Eastern European economies, such as Poland, Hungary and the Czech Republic, the vital force behind their transformation into successful free-enterprise societies has been the spontaneous growth of small business. For example, in Poland in mid-1995 there were about three million small and medium-sized enterprises operating, generating 50 per cent of GDP and 60 per cent of employment. Virtually all these enterprises were new private firms started from scratch rather than products of the programme to privatise assets. Bangkok in Thailand gives you the same impression. When you walk out of the Oriental Hotel, you know you are in entrepreneur-land. Each house on the street has been turned into a manufacturing centre where the sitting room is the sales office and the manufacturing takes place in the backyard. This attitude will do more than anything else to put the country on the "High Road".

South Africa in any case can't avoid becoming a "postmodernist" society which lays emphasis on the service sector. This automatically will lead to the growth of small and microbusiness. It is a tragedy that no serious research has yet been done on the workings of the informal sector. Academics consider it a subject beneath their dignity to study. It is against their ideology to admit that microbusiness is a sun around which other planets revolve. All their attention is given to formulating the rules for the formal sector which one day will be a minority employer. For example, did you know that the minimum effective interest rate being charged to microbusiness by a viable microlending scheme is 39 per cent p.a.? This is the rate of the Start-Up Fund, a remarkable venture based in Cape Town, which lends small sums of money with no security whatsoever. By formal-sector standards the figure sounds usurous, but compare it to the township loan sharks who lend at 50 per cent a month. One black entrepreneur said to me the other day that money was tight and the rate had moved to 100 per cent over the weekend. This is the scale of the going reward for the risks involved in microlending. But returns on capital employed in microbusiness are also much higher than the formal sector. An average hawker expects to make 20 per cent per day. Let's face it! We have no real idea of what is going on in perhaps the most important sector of the economy from the point of view of employment.

The government has recently put a sensible macro-economic strategy on the table. This is the launch pad for economic growth, but it is not the rocket. The rocket is the entrepreneurs and the rocket fuel is venture capital. It would be quite appropriate for Nelson Mandela to say: "I have spent 27 years in jail and since then I have been a politician. I am not a rocket scientist. You people in business know about capitalism and it is therefore up to you to promote it so that it is seen as a popular activity and not a privileged pastime for the few." Somehow, the business sector has to take up the challenge and instil the spark in the young boy kicking a soccer ball in a township street so that he says: "I want to be an entrepreneur – I want to be like Bill Gates" every time he kicks the ball. Little girls should be taught the same.

If South Africa is to succeed in terms of the "rules of the game" outlined for the global scenarios, we will need to create a universal passion for business in this country. Our goal must be a new, energetic and enthusiastic entrepreneurial class with "world-class" aspirations. Having cleared the difficult political hurdle, we mustn't stumble now on the economic one. I don't think we will because South Africans are good at confounding the world. While we don't control the "rules of the game" for the world, we do control our own destiny. It is up to each one of us to choose the path we take. In the words of Pete Seeger, that outstanding 1960s folk singer: "Deep in my heart, I do believe, we shall overcome someday".